5 95

STRONG MEDICINE

History of healing
on the
Northwest Coast

Robert E. McKechnie II, M.D.

1972 / J. J. Douglas Ltd.
Vancouver, B.C.

STRONG
MEDICINE

J. J. DOUGLAS LTD.
3645 McKechnie Drive
West Vancouver

ISBN 0-88894-011-4

Designed, printed and bound in Canada by
MORRISS PRINTING COMPANY LTD.
Victoria, British Columbia

This book is dedicated to my father, *Dr. William C. McKechnie,* who was a family practitioner, beloved by those he served.

ACKNOWLEDGEMENTS

Legend of Siwash Rock, taken from the *Legends of Vancouver*, by Pauline Johnson, reprinted by permission of the Canadian Publishers, McClelland and Stewart Limited, Toronto.

Emily Carr's description of Dr. Helmcken from *The Book of Small* by Emily Carr. Copyright, 1942, by Clarke, Irwin & Company Limited. Used by permission.

CONTENTS

PREFACE

MEDICAL MEN have been closely intertwined in the story of British Columbia. Historical records suggest that a priest-physician of Asia discovered the British Columbia coast and North America a thousand years before Columbus. Legends abound with the colourful doings of the Indian shamans. A surgeon was the first recorded white settler on Vancouver Island and another surgeon gave the world its first description of certain plants peculiar to the Pacific Northwest. Physicians figure prominently in the early legislative bodies of the area.

Yet for all the celebrity attained by these men, the history of the practice of medicine in British Columbia remains poorly documented. Where contemporary historical accounts deal with the pioneer physician, they tend to dwell on his contributions in such extra-medical realms as business, politics or botany. The medical problems he encountered and his methods of caring for the sick with the limited equipment and knowledge at his disposal seem to have been dismissed by the early writers as scarcely worth mentioning. The story must be pieced together from fragments and asides tossed here and there into journals, reports, reminiscences and a whole miscellany of otherwise unrelated writings.

The author has been fortunate in being able to add to these sources a childhood nurtured by tales of the Indians and their physician-shamans, of the coming of the white man's medicine and of the trials and joys of such men as his father, himself a pioneer of medicine on the British Columbia coast.

The locale of this history of early health care is a unique and well defined area that, because of its mild climate and bountiful resources, tended towards high population densities long before the coming of the white man. The area comprises most of what the explorers and fur traders referred to as the Pacific Northwest. It is bounded by the Pacific Ocean to the west and barricaded on the east by the Coast Range, a chain of mountains so rugged it is penetrated only by a few tumultuous rivers and their valleys. Its equable climate is maintained by the warm glow of the Japan Current and it is cut through by thousands of miles of inland waterway, protected from the perils of the open ocean by a string of close-lying islands that extend from the Straits of Juan de Fuca to Alaska. Today the waterway is the delight of the cruising yachtsman and a vital artery of commerce, even as it served the Indian travelling in the dugout canoe of his day.

In addition to the attractions of its rugged setting and its gentle climate, the area abounds in the raw materials of good living. The sea and the rivers yield plentiful supplies of salmon, cod, halibut and shellfish. Game abounds in the forests and a multitude of cedar trees and other conifers provide lumber ideal for building and other domestic purposes. Its resources made it a land of "the good life" in the days of the Indians and their predecessors and it remains so to this day.

It is said that the story of medicine is the story of man. The west coast of Canada is an area well suited to the observation of man's transition from primitive life and Shamanism to modern living and scientific medicine, for here the transition is a matter of recent history. Many of the trees standing in our forests today were thriving before the white man came. When he did come, there was no medicine other than the primitive medicine of the Indian. Into this virgin territory he introduced what little medical knowledge he had, along with such scourges as pestilence and alcohol and moral depravity. During this period, the standards of medical practice in British Columbia were based on the standards of nautical medicine of the Royal Navy or on the traditions of the

Hudson's Bay Company, depending on whether a ship's surgeon or a fur-trading surgeon was providing the care. At a later date, as modern scientific medicine developed, it was the general practitioner who assumed responsibility, only to yield his place in turn to a more sophisticated system of health care.

Throughout the narrative the term medicine will be used in its broadest sense to include all the factors involved in improving the health of the people. Standards of cleanliness (hygiene), the foods that were eaten (nutrition) and the influence of the mind over body function (psychosomatic medicine) are as important in their own sphere as the operations of the surgeon and the potions of the physician are in theirs.

It is all too easy, in this day of radioisotopes and antibiotics, to dismiss the chants and potions of the Indian shaman as so much mumbo-jumbo and the crude tools and often bizarre ministrations of the pioneer physician as cruelly ineffective. Nothing could be more misleading. Each made extensive and judicious use of the knowledge and materials available. Each gave evidence of his skill by producing his small share of what were considered, in their time, miracles of cure. It is the author's hope that the pages that follow will help bring to light the dedication, resourcefulness and colourful existence of these men.

R. E. McK.

PART ONE

The Red Man and the
Medicine of Superstition

I

Emergence

IN THE BEGINNING there were no healers. Man, venturing shyly from the safety of the trees, his brain barely groping toward intelligence, had yet to grasp the lofty logic of specialization. Like other mammals, however, he possessed certain useful instincts. When sickness or injury overcame him, he probably crawled away to a quiet spot and may even have licked his wounds. In the ordinary course of events, he did not defecate in his place of abode. But by far his most potent and useful instinctive response, insofar as it gave impetus to the growth of the arts of life preservation, was fear.

There was fear of his enemies, be they man or beast. There was fear of unexplained and therefore mysterious phenomena — the movement of the sun, the moon and the stars, the voices in the babbling brook, the leaping tongues of searing flame that could mean the comfort of a campfire or the terror of a raging burning forest. There were fearsome noises, fearsome creatures, fearsome feelings, fearsome strangers in his lonely world. And there were fearsome illnesses, injuries, pains. Scrabbling to explain these mysteries and to tame them, he seized on the exaggerated images of his dreams and nightmares and conceived of a world populated by spirits. Like a child that attributes a personality to a doll or toy, he attributed spiritual personalities to the animals, the trees, the mountains, the winds, the sky — anything that had the power to frighten him, or to dispel his fright. To these spiritual personalities were added the spirits he believed must be released at the awesome and mysterious advent of death. Little by little, he evolved his first religion, that of animism. It postulated a world filled with spirits, each of which had the power to affect his life either for good or for evil.

It seems inevitable, at least in retrospect, that someone soon would come along who believed that he could influence these spirits and who could convince others of his ability. It was certain that, along with his supposed talents for keeping game close at hand and predators at a distance, he would claim the power to drive off the evil spirits that entered the bodies of those who were injured or fell ill. And so the first medicine man came into being.

Clearly, at this point in the history of man, medicine and religion were one. It was a functional union: There is no doubt that faith can lead to cure and each cure achieved by one of the early healers led in turn to other cures among those who were functionally disturbed. Psychosomatic medicine became the first established branch of medicine.

As time went on, the medicine man, on the lookout for practical aids in the dispensation of his magic, happened on such discoveries as the curative properties of certain herbs, the effectiveness of wet compresses when applied to burns, and the preventive value of certain hygienic measures. As civilization advanced and medicine man evolved into priest-physician, much of this accrued knowledge became part of a religious doctrine. (The anti-pollution laws of the Moslems kept the spring water of desert oases pure for many centuries.)

Later, in some portions of the world, as its lore and repertoire of procedures grew, healing began to achieve the status of a separate and secular concern. But progress was slow. Only in the last 200 years or so did the physician begin to turn away from the semi-mystic thinking that had governed his profession for so many centuries.

2

Early Arrivals

WHEN THE EARLY EXPLORERS LANDED on the coast of what was to become British Columbia, they found the natives more advanced culturally than any of the primitive peoples they had encountered in other lands. With tools that were made from stone, metal and horn, they carved and created works of art. They wove beautiful baskets from reeds and fine wool blankets from the wool of the plentiful mountain goat. They made household utensils, trinkets, and even combs for their hair from bone and cedar wood. They used the fibrous bark of the cedar tree to weave baskets, blankets, hats and other articles of clothing. They excelled in fishing and hunting, and their codes of behaviour might well have caused their white brethren to hang their heads in shame. It would appear that their "medicine making" was on a similarly high level, primarily as a result of the skills of the shaman who was, for his time, a well indoctrinated and trained individual.

Evidence continues to be unearthed that many of these cultural skills were the result of a rather more widespread interchange of knowledge among the inhabitants of the various continents than has generally been supposed. There is little doubt that over the years many strangers visited the Americas, each one leaving behind traces of his culture and customs. It must also be assumed that these visitors were not celibates and foreign genes were added, with pleasure, to those mementos left behind. This intermittent exchange of customs, cultures and genes had resulted in the formation of an identifiable ethnographic group in the Pacific Northwest, composed of many tribes distinct in physical characteristics and languages but with many cultural attributes in common.[1] Their arts and industries, their customs and beliefs differ so much from those of other Indians that they form one of the best defined cultural groups on the continent.

Barricaded as they were from eastern visitors by the mountains, most of the outside influences on the coast resulted from a widely spaced but steady series of contacts with Asiatic visitors. That the Asiatic influence predominated is evidenced not only in many legends of the coast people, but in their rituals, customs and beliefs, as well. A study of their songs and dirges, for example, has revealed many similarities to those of Tibet and China. Marius Barbeau sums up the position by stating, "The ethnological unity of the Siberians and the North Americans is now admitted by all who have made an exhaustive study of the subject."

There is some medical evidence of the Siberian origin of the American Indians. Marius Barbeau has pointed out the frequency of the so-called Mongolian Spot among Indian children born on this continent, and Dr. George E. Darby has confirmed the incidence of the spot among the coastal tribes. Unfortunately, the prevalence of the dark pigmented area in the skin of the backside of the children is common to all dark-skinned races and so can only be used as presumptive evidence of the American Indian's Siberian origin. There is, however, another and more specific linkage between the two groups — the inherited characteristic of their ear wax. Caucasians and Negroes have an 80% or greater probability of having a honey coloured, wet, sticky ear wax, whereas the American Indian mimics the Mongoloid's 90-95% tendency toward a characteristically dry, gray, brittle "rice bran" type of cerumen.

In addition to such evidence, there are several specific reports of Asiatic visitors to the coast. They are interesting not only

6

because of the information they contain but as evidence that similar but undocumented voyages may well have taken place.

The earliest voyage on record is a visit by a group of Buddhist priests who were reported to have arrived in the year 458 A.D. In 499 A.D., the last of these priests was reported to have returned to Asia. His name was Hoei-Shin[2] (sometimes called Hwai-Shan) and his home was Cophene, identified as a town in Afghanistan. His report is incorporated in the official yearbook of the Chinese Empire of that year and in it he describes the Kingdom of Fusang (a region that Captain Cook's charts placed in the vicinity of Vancouver) as a land well organized and ruled by a "King" assisted by his noblemen. It is also recorded that Hoei-Shin introduced Buddhism to Fusang.

There has been some conjecture as to the identity of the first physician to touch land in the Pacific Northwest. This honour has been awarded in the past to Georg Steller, the surgeon on the ill-fated Bering Expedition, sponsored by the Russian government, that got as far as Alaska in 1741. However, as Buddhist priests in the time of Hoei-Shin attended not only to the spiritual needs of the people but to their physical ailments, as well, the term for Buddhist priest was considered synonymous with that for physician. Thus, it seems possible to think of Hoei-Shin as bringing honour to the medical profession as the first recorded man from the Old World to have made a voyage of discovery to North America, well before Leif Ericson.

Other journeys, all out of the west, were made and documented during comparatively recent centuries. One such voyage is recorded in the tale of the "Volcano Woman" contained in the collection of Indian legends, *Haida Myths*, compiled by Marius Barbeau. It tells of a small group or tribe that started out in flight from their enemies, apparently in Asia, and ended by coming to North America in search of a better place to live. According to its opening lines:

Six canoeloads of people sailed out of the bitter seas, once long ago. They were on their way towards sunrise. Although they called themselves Fugitives they were really seekers of a warmer clime and a promised land. . . . [3]

It was these "Fugitives" who, according to legend, eventually came to occupy the front rank of at least three seafaring nations of the North Pacific coast — the Tlingits of southern Alaska, the Tsimsyans of the mainland south of the Portland Canal and the Haidas of the Queen Charlotte and Prince of Wales islands. Inevitably, their culture and customs were introduced and adapted to their new-found homeland.

A more accidental contact with the Orient was afforded occasionally by the Japan Current. This great flow of water did, and still does, bring Asiatic flotsam to the shores of North America, and from time to time this included a manned vessel. Most often the crew members were dead, but occasionally a few survived and remained to add their bit to the way of life of the coastal natives.[4]

The story of such an accidental voyage is given in the records of the Hudson's Bay Company brig *Llama*,[5] sent in 1834 to rescue three sailors who had been blown across the Pacific in a junk loaded with crockery of the flower-pot and willow-pattern design and finally wrecked off Cape Flattery. They were taken as slaves by the Indians and, after rescue by Captain McNeal, repatriated by way of England to the Orient.

A Question of Cleanliness

It took centuries for the Coast Indian to accept healing and
its folklore as a separate art. Once he did, medical legends began
to accumulate and all attempts to intercede with the spirits,
whether successful or not, whether made by the individual tribesman or by the specially endowed and powerful shaman, were
known as "making medicine."

To explain any unusual event — good or bad — the Indian
applied a primitive type of "cause and effect" reasoning. He
believed that "something" had been contacted, consumed or
observed that was possessed of the spirit that caused the event.
That "something" should either be avoided or cultivated, depending on the desired result. Thus, many parts of the daily life of
the Indian revolved around his ritualistic efforts to make medicine
that would keep the evil spirits away and encourage the presence
of good spirits that might protect and help him. Many of these
efforts had no practical effect. Others can be interpreted as crude
attempts at practical medicine. Both types of custom may be seen
illustrated in the conditions that governed the life of a pregnant
woman.

If, for example, she looked at a bullhead, the child would be
as ugly as one. No one in the house of a pregnant woman might
look at things outside through the doorway. He must go outside
and look at them and, if he happened to forget and broke this

rule, he must go outside and turn around once to the left and then go in again. She must not eat cormorant because, if she did, the child would defecate all the time. (The association of eating a guano-proliferating cormorant and a baby's suffering from infantile diarrhea would seem logical to many a primitive mind.) If she ate abalone the child would have its neck turned around. (Wryneck — was this a *post hoc propter hoc* association of ideas that occurred when a pregnant woman ate some abalone and produced a baby with a wry neck?)

On the other hand, there were some practical customs. At Nootka, after the birth of a child and as soon as the afterbirth was thrown off, the woman ran to the sea and "swam with great resolution."[1] She was then given an undoubtedly welcome hot drink. She had to be still and do no work for ten days and to wear a broad woven cedar bark belt around her middle. She then was to take a bath and, for six weeks after, bathe daily in the stream. The afterbirth was disposed of hygienically by being taken away and hung on the branch of a tree. The umbilical cord was satisfactorily treated by being cut with a knife and tied with something soft, such as rabbit or squirrel hair, and smeared with pitch. The newborn was washed in warm water in which spruce bark had been boiled to help make the child strong in after years. The bit of umbilical cord, after dropping off, was sewed up in a piece of ornamented buckskin, with small stones, the dried black part of a fawn's hoof and some small bone beads. This was then attached to the head of the baby's cradle where it jingled pleasantly when the cradle was rocked, a primitive version of the "mobile" so often recommended today to attract the baby's attention and quicken his interest and development. If that piece of dried cord was lost, it was thought the child would be foolish.

As a "pacifier" the infant was often given a piece of fat meat to suck. The meat was tied to the baby's big toe with a buckskin thong, so that if it was partially swallowed and causing choking, the baby's convulsive kicking would pull it out. Some babies were kept in cradles suspended from a flexible pole planted in the ground and rocked by means of a thong that was hooked around the mother's toe.

As soon as the child was born, the father stepped to the doorway and fired an arrow in the air (surely a practice to be commended as less barbarous than today's customary passing out of cigars).[2]

As our understanding of what constitutes healthful living has grown, so has our respect for the habits of life and standards of health achieved by the coastal Indian. The early white visitors, suspicious of any way of life that did not conform to their own often questionable customs, were not so impressed, and their reports tended to be derogatory. As these reports contained the only information available at the time about the health and hygiene of the Indians, the conclusions established in the minds of the Europeans who read them were that the Indians were a primitive, unclean race and that their cultural achievements were negligible.

The first reports to reach Europe followed Captain Cook's landing at Nootka, on Vancouver Island, in 1778. At that time, he and his officers commented in their journals on the "filthy" appearance of the natives, their lack of cleanliness in their communal houses, and the "stench" that pervaded everything and extended everywhere. Cook, a meticulous hygienist aboard his windswept and well aired ship, must have been particularly offended.

A close examination of the explorers' journals reveals much detailed information concerning the living conditions of the natives, and the unbiased reader quickly begins to suspect that, for the Indians, there was a purpose behind the supposed "filth." Practices that appeared unforgivable to European sensibilities were, in fact, elaborations of a well established culture.

From the records it seems that the Nootka men in summer wore a scanty type of cloak hung from their shoulders. This was so sparse that it exposed much of their body and, at times, even "their privities." Their skin was "grimy" and it was difficult to determine its colour, because of the heavy overlay of "filth." The hair was matted with clay and whale oil and tied in a club at the back, or allowed to hang in strings held together by the clay. The women were dirtier than the men and their hair was particularly grimy. Although they wore the same general type of clothing as the men, they took great care to keep their "privities" covered at all times.

Both men and women applied a pomade of whale grease to their bodies, face and hair and then dusted themselves all over with a red powder made from "oker" (ochre), a clay that contained iron oxide. In addition, they used a machine that was apparently analogous to a powder puff to dust themselves with a finely powdered charcoal made from burned cedar wood. On special occasions some of them also carried birds' down in bags and applied it to their heads from time to time with the same machine.

They apparently considered these applications to be an integral part of their costume and the native girls applied an extra amount, seemingly as a beauty aid, before presenting themselves aboard ship to be wooed by the sailors. They were astonished and concerned as to what manner of men these sailors were when their chosen squires put them in a tub and scrubbed them with soap and water to remove their make-up before proceeding with the love making.

It seems clear that the "dirt" that gave the Indians their "filthy" appearance was applied deliberately. Quite possibly, the original purpose was occult and had become obscured by an overlay of time and tradition during many centuries of usage. One might speculate, too, that the charcoal powder was used for its propensity to absorb odours, in those days before commercial deodorants took over.[3] It would seem reasonable, as well, that the charcoal and the decorative red clay could have been applied as a protection against the elements and the ever present swarms of mosquitoes and other insects that plague the area to this day.[4] The liberal application of the clay to the hair might be construed as a measure to discourage the presence of small unwelcome visitors.

The "stench" that was so stressed by the early journal-keepers was undoubtedly unpleasant. The smell of dead fish on a summer's day can be most repulsive to those who come in contact with it only occasionally. The Indians, on the other hand, lived with the smell constantly. They used smelly whale oil liberally on their bodies along with the mud, ate smelly oolichan fish oil daily as a sauce, consumed fish and fishy-smelling whale meat as a staple and, near their villages, maintained trenches in which thousands of oolichans were rotted for their oil. Fish smells were a fact of ordinary life to which the Indians had long since grown insensitive.

The primitive Indans' standards of sanitation were not as high as those of the most civilized Europeans of the day. But were the credentials of the critics so good as to justify their derogatory judgments? And were their remarks based on reasoned and balanced conclusions drawn after a thorough study of the facts? Some of the critics of the Indians were masters of ships that arrived at Nootka with crew members suffering from scurvy, a disease that had already proved preventable. Its presence on board tended to indicate an unhygienic ship commanded by a skipper who was thus himself open to criticism.

The Europeans should have been inured to some dirt and smell. Toward the end of the eighteenth century garbage collection and sewage disposal were pretty rudimentary in most English cities, and the cry of "gardy loo" (*gardez l'eau*), made famous by Hogarth's picture of the dumping of a chamber pot from a bedroom window onto the street and passersby below, was still to be heard throughout the land. The stinking messes were cleaned up daily by street cleaners and this tended to diminish the smells to a tolerable level. However, the street cleaner often refused to work on the Sabbath and the filth created a stench on a warm day that undoubtedly surpassed that of the Indian communities.

A later account of the health and cleanliness of the Indians, though it tended to damn with faint praise, showed more discernment. Albert Parker Niblack, in his report for the U.S. National Museum in 1888 on the "Coast Indians of Southern Alaska and Northern British Columbia," stated "that in bathing and attempts at body cleanliness — Northern Indians — of the Pacific Northwest compared favourably with any other people in the world in comparable temperate zones, but their ignorance of the simplest laws of health is childlike and lamentable." It is an interesting statement. His remarks about Indian standards of body cleanliness give some sign of an ability to consider an alien culture on its own terms. However, the gap between his idea of health care in his civilized state and that of the Indians was so wide that he apparently could not restrict his judgments to their cultural context.

The health care system of the coastal Indians, remarkable as it was, was handicapped by the absence of a written language. All knowledge, medical and otherwise, was handed down by word of mouth from one generation to the next. This verbal method of passing on information lacked the cumulative power of the written word which, particularly in medicine, permits painstaking comparisons that result in progressively constructive diagnostic and therapeutic refinements.

The Indian's method of recording a significant event was to weave a legend about it. Being superstitious, many of his legends involved the spirits and their activities. Those that today would be called medical legends usually told of the spirits of plants, animals, or the dead who were believed to be capable of causing or curing specific illnesses.

Because their classification of a disease was based on its symptoms rather than its etiology, the legends could be confusing and, at times, even contradictory. Thus, there were a number of legends that were used empirically for the eradication of the bad spirits that caused an illness classified comprehensively as "pains in the stomach." It was left to the luck of the sick Indian as to whether the legend chosen for his cure dealt with the ailment from which he actually suffered. One can easily picture the catastrophic result of treating according to a "pain in the stomach" legend suitable for gall bladder disease a patient actually afflicted with acute appendicitis.

In spite of the handicaps, the Indians developed many ritualistic customs that tended towards a healthier way of life. As has been seen, bathing played a prominent ceremonial role in that life. They believed that, when they were fresh and clean and the human smell was gone, the spirits were free to come to them and warn of approaching dangers. Young people preferred to bathe in fresh water and did so every morning or evening. The older people bathed regularly in the sea, particularly those who were ill, and many of the latter lived close to the water to facilitate this treatment of their infirmities.

Bathing was also considered a purification rite. A legend that illustrates the close relationship between tribal law and hygiene is recounted in Pauline Johnson's *The Legends of Vancouver*.[5] It is one of several about Siwash Rock, a prominent rock pillar with a stunted conifer growing at a jaunty angle from its top that is a landmark at the entrance to Vancouver Harbour:

It was thousands of years ago (All Indian legends seem to begin in extremely remote times) that a handsome boy chief journeyed in his canoe to the upper coast for the shy little northern girl whom he brought home as his wife. Boy though he was, the young chief had proved himself to be an excellent warrior, a fearless hunter, and an upright, courageous man among men. His tribe loved him, his enemies respected him, and the base and mean and cowardly feared him.

The customs and traditions of his ancestors were a positive religion to him, the sayings and the advices of the old people were his creed. He was conservative in every rite and ritual of his race. He fought his tribal enemies like the savage that he was. He sang his war songs, danced his war dances, slew his foes, but the little girl wife from the north he treated with the deference that he gave his own mother, for was she not to be the mother of his warrior son?

The year rolled round, weeks merged into months, winter into spring, and one glorious summer at daybreak he wakened to her voice calling him. She stood beside him, smiling.

"It will be today," she said proudly.

He sprang from his couch of wolf skins and looked out upon the coming day: the promise of what it would bring him seemed breathing through all his forest world. He took her very gently by the hand and led her through the tangle of wilderness down to the water's edge, where the beauty spot we moderns call Stanley Park bends about Prospect Point. "I must swim," he told her.

"I must swim, too," she smiled with the perfect understanding of two beings who are mated. For to them the old Indian custom was law — the custom that the parents of a coming child must swim until their flesh is so clear and clean that a wild animal cannot scent their proximity. If the wild creatures of the forest have no fear of them, then, and only then, are they fit to become parents, and to scent a human is in itself a fearsome thing to all wild creatures.

15

So those two plunged into the waters of the Narrows as the gray dawn slipped up the eastern skies and all the forest awoke to the life of a new, glad day. Presently he took her ashore, and smilingly she crept away under the giant trees. "I must be alone," she said, "but come to me at sunrise; you will not find me alone then." He smiled also, and plunged back into the sea. He must swim, swim, swim through this hour when his fatherhood was coming upon him. It was the law that he must be clean, spotlessly clean, so that when his child looked out upon the world it would have the chance to live its own life clean. If he did not swim hour upon hour his child would come to an unclean father. He must give his child a chance in life; he must not hamper it by his own uncleanliness at its birth. It was the tribal law — the law of vicarious purity.

As he swam joyously to and fro, a canoe bearing four men headed up the Narrows. These men were giants in stature and the stroke of their paddles made huge eddies that boiled like the seething tides.

"Out from our course!" they cried as his lithe, copper-colored body arose and fell with his splendid stroke. He laughed at them, giants though they were, and answered that he could not cease his swimming at their demand.

"But you shall cease!" they commanded. "We are the men (agents) of the Sagalie Tyee (God), and we command you ashore out of our way!" (I find in all these Coast Indian legends that the Deity is represented by four men, usually paddling an immense canoe.)

He ceased swimming, and lifting his head, defied them. "I shall not stop, nor yet go ashore," he declared, striking out once more to the middle of the channel.

"Do you dare disobey us," they cried, "we, the men of Sagalie Tyee? We can turn you into a fish, or a tree, or a stone for this; do you dare disobey the Great Tyee?"

"I dare anything for the cleanliness and purity of my coming child. I dare even the Sagalie Tyee Himself, but my child must be born to a spotless life."

The four men were astounded. They consulted together, lighted their pipes and sat in council. Never had they, the men of the Sagalie Tyee, been defied before. Now, for the sake of a little unborn child, they were ignored, disobeyed, almost despised. The lithe young copper-colored body still disported itself in the cool waters; super-stition held that should their canoe, or even their paddle blades touch a human being their marvelous power would be lost. The handsome young chief swam directly in their course. They dared not run him down; if so, they would become as other men. While they yet counselled what to do, there floated from out of the forest a faint, strange, compelling sound. They listened, and the young chief ceased his stroke as he listened also. The faint sound drifted out across the waters once more. It was the cry of a little, little child. Then one of the four men, he that steered the canoe, the strongest and tallest of them all, arose and, standing erect, stretched out his arms towards the rising sun and chanted, not a curse on the young chief's disobedience, but a promise of everlasting days and freedom from death.

"Because you have defied all things that came in your path we promise this to you," he chanted; "you have defied what interferes with your child's chance for a clean life, you have lived as you wish your son to live, you have defied us when we would have stopped your swimming and hampered your child's future. You have placed that child's future before all things, and for this the Sagalie Tyee commands us to make you forever a pattern for your tribe. You shall never die, but you shall stand through all the thousands of years to come, where all eyes can see you. You shall live, live, live as an indestructible monument to clean Fatherhood."

The four men lifted their paddles and the handsome young chief swam inshore; as his feet touched the line where sea and land met, he was transformed into stone.

Then the four men said, "His wife and child must ever be near him; they shall not die, but live also." And they, too, were turned into stone. If you penetrate the hollows in the woods near Siwash Rock, you will find a large rock and a smaller one beside it. They are the shy little bride-wife from the north, with her hour-old baby beside her. And from the uttermost parts of the world vessels come daily throbbing and sailing up the Narrows. From far trans-Pacific ports, from the frozen North, from the lands of the Southern Cross, they pass and repass the living rock that was there before their hulls were shaped, that will be there when their very names are forgotten, when their crews and their captains have taken their long last voyage, when their merchandise has rotted, and their owners are known no more. But the tall, grey column of stone will still be there — a monument to one man's fidelity to a generation yet unborn — and will endure from everlasting to everlasting.

Skeptics will dismiss this legend as unvarnished myth. Others will, perhaps, interpret it as an example of a tribal custom that developed as the tribes gradually recognized that bathing before a birth would tend to minimize the contamination of a newborn baby by its primitive living parents. It is worth noting that, at about the time this legend was recorded, a Scottish woman was convicted of witchcraft because she had cured several children of severe illness simply by washing them.

In addition to bathing, the Indians took many other hygienic measures. They did not brush their teeth — the toothbrush had yet to be invented — but they did wash their mouths out daily before the first meal. After a meal, they used a split cedar toothpick to clean between their teeth. The hair on their heads was allowed to grow long, but the young men pulled out their beards, using their fingers or clam shells to do so. For whatever reason, the women did likewise to their pubic hair. The older men allowed their beards to grow until they became full and bushy. Babies were washed in lukewarm water.

Little is said about childbirth other than to suggest that a difficult delivery "may be helped by the hand."

The Indians were very conscious of their elimination processes and regulated their bowels carefully. One prescription for constipation recommended the use of the heated sap from the blisters of the bark of the balsam tree mixed with catfish oil (essentially the mixing of an irritant and an emollient to make a laxative); one small mussel shellful was taken in the morning before breakfast and another shellful in the evening. For diarrhea, hard food was eaten because it was said to harden the passages. No clams or fish or dried berries were to be eaten. Dog salmon and dried halibut were permitted. As a medication the bark of the fir tree was burned and the coals pulverized and mixed with water. It was said that its efficacy was due to the fact that the fir bark dries up everything upon which it falls.

The Indians did not relieve themselves too close to their living quarters. Some were even said to have privies. In lieu of toilet tissue, flat split cedar sticks were whittled thin and used for cleaning purposes. The whittling of the toilet sticks was often done by the old men of the tribe and, until recent times, it was a source of embarrassed amusement to those in the know when a woman passenger on a coastal steamer saw these sticks being whittled by some old gaffer on the dock and innocently inquired as to what they were to be used for.

4

A Dietary Supplement

THE STATE OF NUTRITION of the Indians was apparently a variable one. Although food supplies were, in general, fairly plentiful in both the forests and the seas, the Indians depended primarily on the periodic runs of salmon that ascended the rivers and streams in uncountable hordes. They did dry and smoke some of the fish for future use, but for the most part the Indians tended to live from day to day. This reliance on fish for food, plus their relative improvidence, led to nutritional imbalances and even to starvation at times.

In this connection, it is worth considering the role that the oolichan, a small fish of the smelt family, played in the diet of the coastal Indians and, to some extent, the interior Indians, as well. The oolichan lives in the sea and swims up the streams to spawn. It is an extremely oily fish and the oil, although it contains no Vitamin A or D (usually common in fish), is rich in other nutritional elements. The Indians caught these fish by the thousands and placed them in trenches, where they were allowed to decay. The carcasses were then put in containers with water that was brought to a boil by the immersion of hot stones. The precious oil could then be skimmed off. When a high-quality product was desired, it was boiled again, and the skimming repeated. After all of this, the oil was placed in a cool area where it solidified to the consistency of butter and was called "h'oolichan grease" by the guttural-tongued Indians. It was prized both as a food and as a source of energy, being used as a sauce on nearly every dish in Indian cuisine. It was valuable also as an article of trade with the tribes of the interior, where oolichans were not available.

The oolichan grease may well have served as a necessary corrective in the Indians' one-sided diet. The idea is supported by early missionaries. According to accounts, those teaching at the mission schools felt that they had to permit the children to bring the oily blobs, complete with strong fishy reek, along with their lunches. When an attempt was made to deprive the children of their due portions, they were observed to fail physically.[1]

Whatever the reason for the oolichan's popularity, the extracting of its oil seemingly has been going on for hundreds of years. B. A. McKelvie reports on a sixth-century Chinese account of the land of Wan Shan which contains an apparent description of one of these trenches filled with thousands of dead oolichans, their oil separating off and their silvery scales floating to the top.[2] McKelvie's translation of the Chinese record would seem far more logical than two previous translations of the document that interpreted the trenches as being filled with "silver water" or "quick silver."

Practical Therapeutics and Alien Spirits

SURGERY WAS PRACTISED by certain members of each tribe who were specially skilled in their art. Socially, they ranked no higher than other craftsmen and held no special position in the hierarchy of the community. They were not permitted by custom to amputate a foot, although sometimes they amputated a finger, using a knife made out of bone. It is presumed that tribespeople who were badly injured or needed a major amputation were allowed to get along as best they could, to die or recover as the gods decreed. This was the custom of primitive peoples throughout the world, there being no place in their economy for the non-productive, whether as a result of injury, illness or age.

Boils and carbuncles were poulticed with a number of different medications varying from the gum of an evergreen tree to a particularly soft and slimy fungus or a paste made of crushed barnacles. If these failed to draw the pus, the one who was skilled in cutting was called and, if he judged the swelling to be ready, he punctured the boil or carbuncle with a sharpened shell or a porcupine quill.

Bad burns were covered with the raw liver of the skate — a treatment that foreshadowed present-day recognition that cod-liver oil can be a useful dressing for burns.

A more remarkable achievement of the Indian was the surgical procedure known as trephining. It was not a common operation, but that it was practised at all is a tribute to the Indian's insight and ingenuity. The evidence is clear in the human skulls found occasionally with an *ante mortem* hole cut through the cranium. Some of those procedures were skillfully carried out, whereas others had the appearance of being poorly done. An example of the former is a skull found in a midden in the Marpole area near the north arm of the Fraser River in 1930 with not one but two holes cut in it. The skull and the deductions made from it are described by Dr. G. E. Kidd, a former professor of anatomy at Kingston. The description is worth quoting, as the age of the skull indicates that sophisticated surgery was being performed in what is now British Columbia as long as two thousand years ago! Dr. Kidd states:[1]

The skull is one of a young adult male. The mandible was found in place, and, from the fact that the lower wisdom teeth were fully erupted while the upper ones were but partially so, his age at death may be fairly accurately placed in the neighborhood of twenty years. The skull is in an excellent state of preservation, the dentition being perfect. The occipital region, as is the case with so many Indian skulls found on the Pacific Coast, is slightly flattened from the pressure of the cradle board, the right side being more so than the left. The cranial capacity is 1441 cc. When found it was partly covered by a thin sheet of copper, and ornamented with dentalium shells, the whole being enclosed in a casing of cedar bark. The copper burial would indicate that the deceased belonged to a family of some importance. The left parietal bone is forced outward, opening the sagittal and left parieto-occipital sutures throughout their entire extent, and to a maximum width of 6 mm. The possible cause of this will be discussed later.

In the occipital region of this skull there are two openings: a larger one situated just above the external protuberance, with its centre slightly to the right of the mid-line, and a smaller one lying two inches lateral to this, directly over the lower end of the right parieto-occipital suture. The larger one is circular, being saucer shaped, with a surface diameter of 40 mm. From here the walls slope inwards to where they cut through the inner table of bone. There the opening is more or less oval in shape, its diameter being 26 mm. and 19 mm. The surrounding bone shows evidence of healing for a period of time extending over some weeks at least.

The smaller opening shows no evidence of healing. The diploe are open, the edges are sharply marked, and scratches made by a cutting instrument are to be seen on the walls. The opening is oval in shape, the long axis being directed up and down. Its dimensions at the surface of the skull are 22 mm. and 13 mm. It barely pierces the inner table at two points, at the upper end by an opening 4 mm. in diameter and at the centre a small hole 2 mm. across. The remainder of the floor is exceedingly thin. This suggests that the operator approached the interior of the skull with great caution, that he had a steady hand and a sharp instrument. This was probably a small spoon-shaped scraping tool, the bone being removed in small shreds or chips. The upper end is undercut while the lower end is bevelled from the surface downwards. This would suggest that he worked from below upwards, the patient's face probably resting on the operator's knee. In the larger opening the reverse is the case, the lower part of the circumference being undercut, suggesting that the scraping was done from above downwards. There are no marks on the skull surface about the opening such as might be made by the instrument slipping.

It seems to be a clear case of antemortem trephining, the larger opening having been made some time prior to and the smaller one immediately before death. The fact that the last-made opening barely perforated the inner table would indicate that the operation was not completed, the probability being that the man died while it was in progress.

In seeking a reason for the trephining, we might consider the open suture line. It may be asked whether a non-malignant tumor, such as glioma, which occurs in young people, is slow growing, and injuries by intracranial pressure could, in a boy of 20 years of age, force open a suture to this extent without causing death. Dr. Pitts, pathologist at the Vancouver General Hospital, is of the opinion that such might be the case. A feature which might explain why the left parietal was forced outward while the right remained in place is the flattening of the skull in the right occipital region. This caused an accentuation of the left parietal eminence, while the right was more widely curved. In this way the pressure would be directed into a cul-de-sac on the left side.

If the tumor theory is correct, we have evidence of an interesting sequence of events. Beginning with headaches increasing in severity, an attempt was made to relieve them by making the larger opening. As the tumor grew, the symptoms became more intense, and a second operation was undertaken, in the course of which the patient died.

There are few reports concerning the treatment of war wounds, although Indian tribes constantly fought with one another. Perhaps such wounds tended to be ignored because they were man-made and thus scarcely worthy of spiritual intervention. David Samwell, Cook's surgeon on the *Resolution*, records an incident following the wounding of an Indian by a sailor. The wound was a penetrating one and had been made by a pike. It was situated on the fleshy part of the arm and Samwell, as a gesture of friendship, took the Indian aboard and dressed the wound. The Indian then left the ship, whereupon two of his friends immediately removed the dressing and placed it in a wooden container. They then took turns sucking the blood from the wound and spitting it carefully into the same container. In all, about a quart was removed over a period of an hour. Why they treated the wound in this way, Samwell did not know, though he suggests the possibility that they thought the pike was a poisoned weapon.

Although the Indians often applied sound practical measures of prophylaxis and cure, as has been described, the theory that all illness was due to supernatural causes remained the dominating influence in their system of health care. According to Dr. S. W. A. Gunn, there were three main theories of pathogenesis:[2]

Spirit sickness. This disease was almost invariably a fatal condition that befell the ritually impure or those believed to have been contaminated by the evil power of an encountered spirit or a witch. The incantations of the specialized shaman and, in some tribes, the help of some small creature such as a mouse were mobilized to oust the evil spirit.

Soul loss. This was a mysterious disease that manifested itself in lethargy and apathy. Apart from his totemic spirits, man was believed to possess a vaguely defined subsidiary soul. The loss of this soul did not cause death outright, but led to a form of psychic and somatic depression which was considered fatal unless treated. Only highly specialized shamans could treat such a disease and an ordinary medicine man would often call his colleagues in consultation. The usual ways of recovering an absentee soul was for these medicine men to send their own souls as well as their helping spirits to search for and fetch the strayed one.

24

Disease by intrusion. Most of the common diseases were believed to be caused by malevolent spirits who sent malicious foreign bodies such as splinters, pebbles, and magical pellets into the body of a person, thus causing him to become ill. The illness could only be cured by the drawing out of this supernatural foreign body and the victim could select one of several approaches to his problem. If his illness was relatively minor, he could try the "home remedy" approach. This involved seeking the advice of his close relatives and friends, or consulting the "Wise Old Woman" of the tribe, or even the local magician, to find the legendary lore that would tell him how to appease the offending spirit. Failing this, he went on to progressively more powerful spirits, the first being the friendly spirit represented in his totem pole. If his totemic spirit was not powerful enough to overcome the evil influence, the victim was forced to seek the costly professional advice of the shaman.

Most of the illnesses that were purported to be helped by placating the spirits were not only severe but, in present-day terms, chronic, and cures were seldom accomplished quickly. To assist the prayers, some practical regulations and treatments were instituted. The requirements of isolation and cleanliness were satisfied by the prescription that the sick person sleep only in his own bed, use his own eating utensils, and have his bucket of water changed three times a day. He was also required to bathe daily at sundown in the belief that he could thus obtain supernatural help from the spirits that were available at dusk. A feverish body was sponged off with cool moist moss and, with the drying of the moss, the evil spirit was said to be released.[3] The hot springs that bubbled out of the ground at various points along the coast were thought to have supernatural powers. Those that contained minerals were considered to be particularly helpful. If the hot springs were not readily available, the patient was steamed over hot rocks covered with kelp and moistened with salt water. After the steam bath the victim was plunged into cold water (sometimes with fatal results). All procedures had to be undertaken in strict adherence to the accompanying legendary ritual. Neglect of even the most minute detail could be taken as the reason for the failure to obtain a cure.

In addition to these hydrotherapeutic procedures, a number of decoctions and ointments were administered that were made from truly medicinal plants. Infusions of poplar or willow bark (containing the glucose salicin, a forerunner of the salycilates) were generally used, as were bearberry (*Arctostaphylos uva-ursi*) for nephritic conditions; False Solomon's Seal (*Vagnera racemosa*) as a uterine stimulant; and shore pine (*Pinus contorta*) in an ointment to relieve aches and pains of rheumatism and sore muscles. James Teit, writing in 1930, lists at least thirty such truly medicinal remedies. Many of these items in the Northwest Indian's pharmacopoeia have proven to be the chemical cousins of the powerful preparations used for similar ailments in modern medicine.

6

The Shaman Takes His Degree

THE INDIAN'S HOME TREATMENT procedures and the skill of his surgeons were potent medicine. They paled into insignificance, however, beside the awesome mystic healing powers of the shaman. He was a fearsome figure, gifted with the ability to intercede with the spirits through a personal spirit-helper that lived inside him. This image he cunningly exploited and enhanced by the use of the closely guarded secrets passed on to him by the older shamans. The common people, bewildered and frightened as they were by their myths and superstitions, were only too eager to become his patients.

The art of the shaman usually was handed down from the maternal uncle to the nephew. Some women became shamans, but the profession was predominantly occupied by males. The candidate selected for the "course" was usually a psychologically sensitive type and was sometimes chosen at an early age. Indoctrination into the cult of the shaman took years and, during that time, the would-be shaman learned many things. He assisted his sponsor at all his "treatments" and soon learned how to evaluate illness. It was of particular importance that he recognize the ailments that he could cure or mitigate; if he failed, the fee that had been paid when he accepted the case had to be returned with consequent loss of face and reputation in his chosen profession. Worse still, if the patient died, he could be suspected of deliberately provoking the offending spirits for his own personal gain, in which event not only would his professional reputation suffer, but he ran the risk of being killed in revenge. In consequence of these risks, the shaman became an exacting judge of illness. He also acquired a detailed knowledge of many remedies that depended for their effect on the patient's faith in the healer. On the other hand, each shaman had some specific practical medicines for such ailments as sore eyes, ulcers and skin conditions that he kept tucked away in his bag of tricks — professional secrets that did much to build his reputation.

To help him practise his own personal brand of Shamanism, the young shaman gathered together and learned to use the tools of his trade. Each item was revealed to him by his personal activating spirit and its particular association with the spirit world identified. A soul snatcher that could be used to snatch back an errant soul that had left the body of his patient was important. A hollow bone tube to suck out the foreign body that had intruded itself into the vitals of the sick one was needed. In addition, many magical items had to be acquired for special purposes known only to himself — an eagle's claw, a seagull's wing, a dessicated bear paw, a bird and a small animal such as a mouse or a weasel — each to be produced and used when their special powers were called for. Having gathered the items he required, he placed them in his ornate and mystical *mesahchie* bag, the deerskin equivalent of the modern doctor's black bag, and took them with him along with the ritualistic drum and rattle wherever his professional services were required.

He studied and perfected the art of psychologically swaying the crowd of relatives and onlookers who had come to see him make contact with the spirit world. To do this convincingly, he learned how to throw himself into a trance, some of the rudiments of hypnosis, and even ventriloquism. To enable him to present concrete evidence of his contact with the supernatural, he cultivated the art of legerdemain to a high level. Thus it was that, when he eventually became a full-fledged shaman and donned his special hat and blanket, with its totemic crest and rabbinical fringes, and went out into the world, he was fully equipped mentally and physically to perform as a master of psychosomatic medicine. What is more, "his strength was as the strength of ten," because he believed in himself implicitly.

After his long apprenticeship in the arts of the shaman, he had one more task to perform before being initiated into the profession. He must make himself "clean" by fasting and privations and, at the same time, he must let his hair grow long and not comb or wash it. Then, having been accepted by one of the spirits of The Above People, The Canoe People, The Ocean People, or other supernatural beings, his spirit would possess him as a means of making its existence known to man. To find this spirit, the neophyte walked over the beaches and through the forests, calling mournfully, to attract the attention of the spirit people. Then, having been possessed by the spirit, he became its mouthpiece, dressing as it directed and speaking the strange language that it spoke. He was then ready for the final rugged ordination ceremony that, if passed successfully, would admit him into the world of the shaman. He was expected to conduct himself through the gruelling rites in a supernatural manner and, under no circumstances, was he to show signs of so human a frailty as pain.

The following description of the indoctrination of a shaman not only tells the story of the cruel physical hardships of the ceremony, but also gives an insight into the life of a practising white physician of the time. It is told by Doctor W. W. Walkem in his book, *Stories of Early British Columbia*, written in 1914. In 1876, Dr. Walkem was the Health Officer for the City of Victoria and had been requested to travel to Comox, 140 miles to the north, to vaccinate the Indians of that settlement "without exception" against smallpox. He boarded the coastal steamer *Cariboo Fly* and three days later arrived at his destination. He had a letter of introduction to Mr. A. G. Horne, who was the chief trader in the Hudson's Bay Company's post on the Indian reservation. Mr. Horne told Dr. Walkem that he would not be able to vaccinate the Indians immediately as "they were," he said, "in a high state of excitement, bordering on frenzy, over the coming ceremonies incidental to the 'making' of a Shaman, or Indian medicine man." Doctor Walkem then proceeded to make friends with the Indian chief, Nim-Nim, and was invited to accompany him to the ordination that was about to take place:[1]

As we walked over he (Nim-Nim) told me of the former importance and numbers of his tribe, and how the deadly smallpox introduced by an Indian who had been in Victoria, and had returned with the disease, had carried off more than five hundred of his Tillicums. Then he would fiercely tell me that it was brought to the country by the white man. Now white men ploughed the fields where they once hunted the wild animals for their meat. They are now confined on reservations, while long ago they moved about where they wished to go. But the Government was good to him, because they knew he was a 'hyas closhe man.'

Thus he poured into my ear the woes and troubles of his tribe. We shortly arrived opposite the entrance of the rancherie. Two planks of three inches in thickness, fastened together by two stout cross pieces led up an inclined plane to the entrance, and as we reached the wall of the building I observed that the footwalk was curved on both edges like the sides of a canoe. Crossing the doorway under the lintel, the footwalk sank down like a see-saw, and the end rested on the ground within the building. As soon as we stepped off the board walk, it rose slowly upwards and stopped with a snap. On looking at it from within, the entrance was fashioned to represent the head of a bald-headed eagle. The planks on which we entered the building filled the place of the lower beak or mandible. We, therefore, came in through the bird's throat.

It was a very clever and ingenious piece of work. The whole head was almost a perfect model of what it was intended to represent. For eyes the Indians had used some large shell, which gave a savage glint, as would be expected to emanate from such a bird. The building itself was not quite so long as the one at Saanich, but it was equal to it in width. This one, however, had a large square opening in the centre of the roof. Over this opening was a square covering raised on four posts about four feet in length. This covering was to prevent the entrance of rain, during the rainy season or at other times. From the ends of four timbers, which were bound firmly together, and projected into the square opening, hung a pulley, attached to the timbers by a stout rope. Another rope ran over the pulley wheel, at one end of which was a long steel hook. The remainder of the rope, which was of considerable length, was coiled on the outside of the roof. All this was explained to me by the chief, and I have described this pulley and the way it was attached to the timbers at some length, as it played a very important part in the functions of the night.

Chief Nim-nim explained to me that it was not a member of his tribe who was to become a Shaman that night, but one Johnny Chiceete, from Cape Mudge, not far from the entrance to Seymour Narrows. Johnny was one of the Yu-kwul-toes, or Yuclataws, as white men usually call the tribe. They were at one time the most blood-thirsty and the most dreaded of the coast tribes. Johnny was compelled to come to Comox for his initiation, as it was the only camp where there were many Medicine Men to take part in the ceremony.

In consideration of this privilege, Johnny intended on the following day giving as a free gift to those assembled for the ceremony, one thousand dollars' worth of goods. This was termed a cultus potlatch, and went to show as well, for the Indian dearly loves boasting, that he had a 'shook-um tum-tum,' and was possessed of 'hy-yu-ictas,' much substance, or to put it in our language — that he was a man of wealth, and gave away for the mere love of it. He wished coute qui coute to have his name noised about as a prince of good fellows. This is the Indian character, on this coast at least.

At this point in this narrative is a good opportunity for me to explain the process through which a novitiate passes in his course to become a full fledged medicine man, which I am enabled to do from a long residence in this province, during which time I have had a great deal to do with Indians and their affairs and customs.

The first movement of the aspirant for medical honors is to take to the woods and find some isolated lonely spot, either on some mountain top or by the waters of some lake, where his cries to his 'temenwos' will not be heard by human ears. All Indian cries are a species of lamentation, and are much the same whether made by the novitiate to his 'temenwos' or by the howler on the sea shore, by the side of some dead body. They are fearfully sad, and striking so weirdly on your ear at dead of night, give you the shivers.

Thirty-three years ago I had to go to the head of the North Arm to see a sick logger. I had hired Big Footed George of Seymour Creek to take me there. As we approached the shore line beneath Temenwos Lake, now called Lake Beautiful, one of these howlers broke out with her dismal lament. George would go no further. He was afraid of the spirits of the lake above. He turned the canoe, notwithstanding my protests, and fled swiftly towards his home on Seymour Creek. I had to engage a white man to take me up next day. It is, or was, very difficult to get a Siwash to take you anywhere at night, unless he was one of the Mission Indians.

When camped on the shores of Lake Buttle some twenty years ago, I was awakened about two o'clock in the morning by a most plaintive wail, which struck upon my ear from a distance which, I judged, was half a mile away. The wailing continued for fully three hours. I recognized it as the plaintive appeal of the future Medicine Man to his temenwos. My companion, a young Irishman not long out from the 'ould sod' would not agree with me as to the reason or cause of the wail. He insisted that it was a 'banshee' for he had heard the same on the Lakes of Killarney, when he was a boy. I smiled, and said no more, for argument was useless. Towards morning the wail of the novitiate was supplemented by the screams of two cougars from opposite sides of the lake. This produced a far greater impression on my young friend than his banshee. He insisted that we should return home on the morrow, as it was a most uncanny place in which to be camped at night. I saw the novitiate the next day. He was almost naked, but stole away into the timber as fast as possible on seeing me. I afterwards learned that he was an Indian from Alert Bay. In their incantations by the lake they are sometimes answered by the laughing quaver of the Great Northern Diver, as though resenting the encroachment of his solitude.

For six weeks or more the 'would-be Shaman' wanders sadly through the mountains picking his sustenance from the berries, or edible tubers which everywhere abound. His nights are wholly consumed in the never-ending appeal to the temenwos, or to those spirits good or evil which may hear his distressing appeals for recognition. They are spiritualists, pure and simple, but their spiritualism differs from the modern 'ism' of the present day, in that the spirit or 'temenwos' whom they appeal to is in their belief an original spirit, and not the spirit of one who has died. Privation and lack of food no doubt reduce the Indian novitiate to a condition bordering on hysteria, and when in that condition he is liable to believe that he hears the answer to his plaintive wails for help and recognition. It is at this stage that he determines to return to the homes of his tribe. He is now dangerous — a species of demon, whose hunger must be appeased by flesh.

Slowly and stealthily he makes his way back to where his former companions are anxiously awaiting his return. When within a short distance of his place of birth, he rushes in with frightful yells, and woe betide the unfortunate native whom he first encounters on his way. He leaps upon him like a wild beast, and probably bites a piece out of his victim's arm. No resistance is offered, as it is considered a great privilege to be thus bitten by the future Shaman. The man is famished and he devours the piece of flesh like a hungry dog. If, instead of meeting with one of his own kind, he sees a dog, he will, if possible seize it with both hands and rend the animal to pieces.

Once outside the village or settlement, four or more sturdy members of the tribe pounce on him and confine him for the last and trying ordeal which I saw in the case of Johnny Chiceete, or grey-haired Johnny, as he was known to the whites. I will describe this shortly.

After parting from Chief Nim-nim at the entrance to the rancherie, I returned to the hotel where I was a guest, and after dinner made my way to the Hudson's Bay post, where I met Mr. and Mrs. Horne, as well as Mr. and Mrs. Alexander Grant, who were the only other whites who were permitted to view the ceremony. As the ceremony was supposed to begin at 7 o'clock we lost no time in hastening to the rancherie. We were accompanied by a large number of Indians from Cape Mudge, and other points, who did not live in the Comox rancherie. As I looked at them, I thought of Cooper's 'The Last of the Mohicans.'

These, too, were among the last of a passing race, whose ranks even from the date of my arrival, had been sadly decimated by smallpox and other diseases. Of course, we did not want to have him with us, dressed out in the panoply of war, stealing stealthily on his neighbors, knife in hand, slaughtering men, women, and children without distinction of age or sex, but we would love to see him leading an industrious life and enjoying that civilization which we had brought him. The Pacific Coast Indian is not fitted by disposition or inclination to take advantage of what is offered to him.

It was still light when we entered the rancherie, two at a time through the eagle's throat. Four Indians with wolf masks over their faces guarded the entry on the inner side. Two other natives with bear and eagle masks stood close to these four. They were all there to see that no interlopers gained admission to the building. Chief Nim-Nim stood a short distance from them, resplendent in scarlet tunic and high silk hat. His hat had received since I saw him in the afternoon three additional eagle feathers to reinforce his dignity and importance as a Chief. The building was well filled with a mixed audience of Indians from up and down the coast.

We were shown to seats well up from the floor, but commanding a perfect view of the whole inside of the rancherie. At intervals along the front were sentinels encased in a complete suit of feathers, their figures being topped by a mask of a most perfect imitation of the bald-headed eagles, and glittering eyes as already described, as completing the eagle head entrance. I noticed that all the women of the tribe were seated well up from the ground floor, and appeared

33

to me to wear upon their faces an aspect of anxiety, if not of fear.

About three-quarters of an hour had elapsed when the drummers in the centre of the ground space began to beat a regular rhythmic stroke upon the gigantic drums which they had before them. Four Shamans were walking up and down in this space, one of whom reminded me of a huge baboon I had seen at the Zoological Gardens in Regent's Park. While singing they were shaking rattles, as well as their ankles, most assiduously, which were adorned with shells and small rattles. In a few moments some of the women and men stepped out upon the floor, and began to move about in the usual dancing step. Their tunes are always the same, and the movements of the dancers also. These dances were kept up for some time, one middle-aged man showed his gastric capacity by swallowing a square gin bottle of dog fish oil without drawing a breath. He subsided in a helpless condition upon the earthen floor, from which he was promptly packed off to one of the platform seats.

At 8 o'clock everything was perfectly quiet, so quiet indeed, that you could have heard a pin drop in the dusty floor. Then a noise, with much howling was suddenly heard proceeding from the roof. In a few moments a human body was pushed through the square hole in the roof of the rancherie. As the body dangled inside the skylight, as I will call it, I was able to see that the figure was pendant by four hooks and chains, from the pulley I have already mentioned as being at the end of the four poles, lying across the skylight. It was the body of Johnny Chiceete which was dangling in the upper air. He was hanging suspended by four hooks, one through the muscles of each upper arm, and one through the muscles of each thigh. He was completely naked, with the exception of a loin covering made from the inner bark of the cedar.

His attendants of the roof lowered him slowly to the ground, then back to the roof and down again. This was repeated three times. While going up and down he shouted out some words which I took to be a species of ritual, for at every pause in his speech he was answered by the Shamans on the ground below. They kept walking up and down in line for about twenty feet and back, silent while Johnny Chiceete was speaking, and picking up the words just as Johnny ceased. No sign on Johnny's face told of the horrible torture he must have been enduring. He could not have been more quiet if he had been lowered and raised in a capacious basket.

At the termination of the third drop, four big powerful members of his tribe rushed out and grasped him by the arms, while the hooks were kept quite taut to prevent his breaking away. Straps were round his arms to give his captors a good firm hold and command

34

of his body. The hooks were then removed, and Johnny sprang to his feet, and attempted to break away.

Many of the audience, fearful he should escape from his captors, began to seek safer positions. Now came the most curious part of the ceremony. Ten Indians came down the circular pathway, naked to the waist. Johnny saw them and began to gnash his teeth in anticipation of a feast, for he was fearfully hungry, having arrived from the mountains a short hour before his appearance on the roof. As Johnny strained like a dog on the leash to get at the first semi-naked Siwash, he seemed more like a wild beast than a human being.

Gradually he dragged his keepers to his first victim, the Shamans following in the rear with pieces or strips of cotton and Indian balm. Arriving at the first man, he seized his arm, and bit a large piece out of it, and then passed on towards the next. The Shamans to our surprise called our special attention to the wound in the first man's arm, to show there was no fake about, I suppose. Then they applied some balm or ointment, and wrapped up the whole in cotton.

After binding up the wound in the first man's arm, a Shaman slipped a ten-dollar gold piece into the victim's hand, according, as I was afterwards told by Mr. Horne, to an arrangement between the victim and Johnny Chiceete's friends. After this performance with his teeth, Mrs. Horne and Mrs. Grant retired from the building. It was too horrible for their sensitive nerves. Mr. Horne, Mr. Grant and I stayed on to see the ceremony through. Johnny completed his round with the hired victims, and just as he finished with the last, he saw a small dog near the platform, which he seized with both hands and began to eat alive. He was pushed, with the dog in his hands, towards the entrance and was taken by his friends to a cabin specially prepared for him, where his hook wounds received special attention. All of those who supplied Johnny with arms to bite were rewarded in the same way as the first one was, who by the way was an Indian known to the whites as Siwash George. I only heard the names of three others. They were Three Fingered Jimmy, Saweetlum and Potato Johnny.

If this represented the ceremony of making an Indian Medicine Man at a time when the province was well settled, what must have been the orgies in connection with the same performance before the whites came.

The late Mr. Moffatt, an old servant of the Hudson's Bay Company, told me when spending the evening with him, in Victoria, that once when stationed at Fort Rupert he saw one of these noviatiates, on his return from seeking his temenwos, run amuck throughout the rancherie, biting men, women and children, and he even attempted to bite Mr. Moffatt, but he felled him with a blow, which the natives thought would be followed by his instant death. The natives consider it a great privilege to be bitten by a novitiate, or rather I should say, they once thought so, but now they must receive compensation for providing the material for the proper carrying out of the ceremony.

After the retirement of Johnny Chiceete, wine made from the ollale (salmon berry) was handed round among the guests.

The last performance was very amusing. Two of the men covered with complete suits of bird plumage, engaged in a fight in the centre of the arena. By some means they opened their beaks and took a bite out of each other's plumage, and then blew feathers into the air through a hole in the top of the head. They imitated the rasping screech of the baldheaded eagle to perfection. Then an encounter took place between a wolf and a bear, which was a tame affair, as they were rather clumsy on their feet.

We left the rancherie at midnight, but we could hear the beating of the dance drums until past daylight.

Next day Johnny Chiceete gave a grand potlatch, when he threw away to his Tillicums, one thousand dollars' worth of goods, consisting of bales of blankets, a cuddy of tobacco, boxes of crackers, barrels of molasses, as Mr. Grant told me to make his friends stick to him, boxes of apples, flour, and not forgetting the red and yellow handkerchiefs so dear to the Siwash heart.

To show his indifference to money values he broke up and burned a new large war canoe, valued at $175.

Dr. Walkem also quotes a similar initiation ceremony, held many years earlier, that was much more brutal in nature. It had been seen and described by the Hudson's Bay factor at Fort Simpson, who was visiting the Russian trading post at Sitka.[2] After being wined and dined most graciously by the Russian governor of the territory, he was taken in to see the ceremony. He states that the initiate was mad with hunger and, without a moment's warning, rushed at one Indian, who happened to have his head turned away at the moment, bit a large piece of flesh out of his arm and swallowed it in a most ravenous manner. He was, after repeating these bites on six or seven other Indians, seized by several stalwarts. Then some shamans advanced and ran skewers made from walrus ivory beneath the deep muscles of the would-be shaman's back. Two of these were used and to each one was attached a rope made from the hide of the walrus. By these ropes the man was hauled up into mid-air over pulleys set on top of the building. Then he was swung backwards and forwards until his seat almost touched the roof, the muscles of his back bulging forward as though some part of the flesh would give way at any moment. The man in the meantime never uttered a sound; this in spite of a number of shamans, dressed in skins of beasts and their heads surmounted with masks denoting ravens, who walked up and down in the central space administering a lash each time the body of the man swung by.

Clearly, the ordination ceremonies of a shaman made a powerful contribution to his mystique. The descriptions of these rites make it all the easier to understand the respect and high position the shaman held in his tribe.

7

A Shaman's Manual of Practice

As is true of present-day practitioners, the shaman was consulted about many problems of tribal and personal significance. Although he was not a chieftain, he had a great influence over the daily lives of the common people. He was consulted about the most propitious times for certain undertakings and was involved in the rites that accompanied them. The killing of the first salmon of the season, the collecting of the first berries, and the cutting down of a cedar tree to make a canoe — all these had to be carried out according to proper ritualistic form. It was important, for example, to maintain a good relationship between the spirit of the salmon and the tribespeople by respectfully explaining to the salmon spirit that the Indian killed the fish only because he needed the food so that he would not starve to death. Before a war party set out, the shaman's spirit was sent ahead to ensure disaster for their enemies. A new community hall required his services, as did many other public works projects. The spirits were everywhere and the shaman must constantly intercede to prevent them taking offence.

To assist the shaman with any medical problems that might arise, he had been provided, as has been described, with a sizable fund of practical knowledge. Most of it was gathered during his apprenticeship; the remainder was acquired through his experience in actual practice. His facility in the recognition of various types of illness, the psychology of man, the use of legerdemain, ventriloquism, hypnotism and other such expertise were props to be produced when the opportune moment arrived. In addition, he had a number of personally compounded decoctions and salves to prescribe for certain specific conditions. Many of these would today be classified as nostrums, but others must have been startlingly effective. Any cures obtained were assisted not only by the detailed ritualistic instructions that accompanied the remedies, but also by those important mainstays of all pre-scientific medicine — faith, hope and the recognition by the Shaman that time is the healer of many things.

Even a modicum of improvement was considered as a great success by those involved and well worth the effort and expense put into the cure. The alternative to that modicum of improvement could be drastic or even hopeless. Usually it meant the patient must resign himself to suffer stoically whatever ailment or injury had befallen him, consoling himself only with age-old fatalism of "what will be will be." By and large, the sufferers accepted their fate but, as from time immemorial, there were some strong aggressive individuals who refused to bow down to their illness and searched the coast for a shaman who could help them. This not only tended to give rise to competitive Shamanism but also served to implement the evolutionary axiom of "the survival of the fittest."

When a shaman was asked to see a tribesman suffering from a serious illness, it was most often an illness that fell into his classification of "soul sickness" or "disease by intrusion." All seriously ill people were a challenge to his art, his reputation, perhaps even to his own good health, so it was important that he refuse those he could not help. He made a preliminary visit to the patient not only to decide whether or not to accept the case but also to assess the lay of the land and plan the staging of his curative procedures. Having decided to proceed, he then collected his fee. This at times reached grand proportions, for his personal contact with the spirit world made him a man who must not be offended. Rich furs, slaves, canoes and other such valuables were considered fitting gifts — to be returned, of course, in the event of a failure to produce results.

The shaman then left to think about and organize his attack on the offending spirits. In a serious case involving an important man of the village he might call in one of his confreres in consultation. Then, having planned his procedures, he arrived at the communal house carrying his magical *mesahchie* bag and dressed in the regalia of his profession. He was usually accompanied by one or more assistants carrying the ceremonial drums and other ritualistic paraphernalia. One can picture them as they enter the great room, with its fire burning in the centre. The spectators and relatives are awestruck. All eyes are on the shaman, the man who is possessed by his own personal spirit. It is his show, compounded and supported by the superstition, fear and ignorance of his audience and his patient.

The procedures the shaman employed differed, depending on such circumstances as the tribe involved, the severity of the illness, the skill of the shaman and, undoubtedly, the wealth and prominence of the patient. Some intercessions took little time; others lasted for days. Often relatives or close friends were asked to participate.

In a typical ritual, those involved start by drinking salt water as an emetic and bathing, to cleanse themselves inside and out before exposing themselves to the spirits who are to come. They fast even though the performance may last for several days. When the mood has been set by these preliminaries, the shaman begins a slow dance around the fire, keeping his left hand towards the centre of the house. He rattles his rattle and his assistants rhythmically beat their drums and everyone keeps up a continuous chant. Volume and tempo are carefully modulated, for the shaman has an eye on the mood of his audience. Gradually, he builds up a frenzy in himself that affects the others in the room, much as the revivalist's rising exhortations wring a growing response from his susceptible flock to this day.

The shaman circles closer to the sick one, touches him with his hands, massages the affected part, blows air at it through his hollow bone tube, snatches for the errant soul with his soul snatchers, meanwhile never ceasing his secret incantations. He waves over the patient his sacred amulet, a special gift to him from his spirit to help in affecting the cure. Finally, his frenzy reaches such a pitch that it is clear to all that the shaman's personal spirit has taken him over. The superstitious, impressionable centre of all this activity is completely terrified by now and, when the shaman in a final fearsome frenzy descends on him and sucks through his bone tube and magically produces and shows him the offending intrusive body, whether it be pebble, splinter or whatnot, the victim's psyche and his somatic systems are so shocked that any cure that the power of mind over body could possibly effect is promptly effected.

8

The Power Wanes

SHAMANISM IS NOT AN ORIGINAL AMERICAN WORD. It was primarily the cult of spirits and ancestral ghosts practised by the Ural-Altaic peoples of Asia and northeastern Europe — the Finns, Hungarians, Turks, Mongolians and Tungus. Shamanism existed in Tibet before the coming of the Buddhist religion. Marius Barbeau has made comparative studies that reveal a close resemblance between the Shamanistic practices in British Columbia and those in Tibet. But none of its venerable history could save Shamanism from the onslaught of European civilization.

Slowly, after the arrival of the white man and the raising of the "cedar curtain" by the accompanying men of science, the shaman began to acquire a reputation as a faker and a charlatan. His secret incantations, his soul snatcher and his magic tube appeared more and more to be hocus pocus in the cold light of reason and he began to lose his hold on his people.

All the same, old customs die slowly. In remote areas, where the white man's magic was slow to penetrate, the Indian continued to turn to his shaman in times of trouble. During the great influenza epidemic of 1918 and 1919 there were not enough doctors to go around and many Indians depended on their shamans for help.[1] In the remote village of Kispayaks on the upper Skeena River, a shaman by the name of Nooks magically created the figure of a female medicine woman and she was credited with saving many lives.

Inevitably, civilization with its enlightenment closed in around the shaman. The death throes of his art are reflected in the last witchcraft trial, held in March of 1931. Alex Tye, an Indian over 80 years of age, and Donald Grey were the accused, charged with having claimed to have taken the troublesome spirit of a bear out of the throat of one Tye David Francis and blown it away. They were convicted, but their one-year suspended sentences suggest that their transgressions were no longer taken very seriously.[2] Thus, a century and a half after his arrival, the white man presided over the demise of a tradition that had taken millennia to perfect.

Cannibalism frequently has been mentioned as a concomitant of the Shamanistic rites.[3] F. W. Howay, writing of the impressionable years of exploration, states categorically that no proven case of cannibalism ever came to his attention. A possible explanation for the persistence of the rumours is given by Assistant Commissioner (retired) Clark of the British Columbia Provincial Police. He concludes that the white man, gullible enough to believe in cancer-curing ointments, to don electric belts for the relief of rheumatism and to argue fiercely that the automobile would never replace the horse, could be taken in by anything. He cites the experience of Dr. C. E. Newcombe, who took five Indians to the St. Louis World's Fair in 1904. Dr. Newcombe was a well known writer and an authority on the Coast Indians, but was nevertheless taken in completely by the myths. He had to be told by the shamans to more or less mind his own business when he tried to stop them from apparently killing and eating a small Negro boy. The audience at the Fair was equally shocked and only satisfied that murder and cannibalism had not taken place before their eyes when the little boy was produced, healthy and well, not a morsel missing from his body.[4]

One may wonder whether the replacement of the shaman with the noble practices of the white man's magic has had a beneficial effect on the Indian nations. Doubtless, a complex of influences and events has been at work. The fact remains, however, that in the shaman's time, the population of the Indians numbered one hundred to one hundred and fifty thousand. Today, it is only about one-third of that number.

At the time that Hoei-Shin was said to be visiting the Pacific Northwest, Shamanism was well established. About the same time, European Christians were listening to the words of St. Augustine and others, who attributed illness to the diabolical influence of the demons. Medicines were considered useless. The only hope of cure resided in ridding the sick one of his demons by the laying on of hands and the prayers of holy people. In the circumstances, it may be conceded that the Indian's medicine-man — the shaman — served his people well.

PART TWO

The Early Medicine
of the White Man

9

A Spicy Beginning

UNTIL THE MIDDLE OF THE SIXTEENTH CENTURY, the Pacific Northwest was largely unknown territory to the European and he marked it conveniently on his global charts as "Terra Incognita." There were speculations and assumptions about the presence of some land masses in the form of islands somewhere between Europe and Asia, but little was known and, most likely, less was cared.

It was about 1564 A.D. that interest was aroused in this unknown region by a chart published by a cartographer named Abraham Ortelius. In it, he consolidated some assumptions, some known facts and, we may conclude, some imaginative flights of a cartographer's fancy. Labrador was shown as an island and the northern shore of North America was at the level of the British Columbia-Yukon border at 60° north latitude. There was an immense Mare Selentrionale which was shown to communicate with the Pacific Ocean via the Straits of Anian. The latter had been vaguely described by Marco Polo in the year 1295 A.D., as he looked eastward from the Asiatic shore of the Chinese province of Anian. These straits represented the first conception of what was to become popularly known as the Northwest Passage to the Orient, a phantom that would be the object of a vigorous search, from both the Atlantic and the Pacific sides, during the next two and one-half centuries. Thirteen years after Ortelius published his chart, Queen Elizabeth I gave Sir Francis Drake, as one of his commissions, instructions to sail to the western coast of North America and find any east-west waterway that might exist. He was, of course, to claim for England any new territory he might happen across in the process. Drake did sail northward in the Pacific Ocean and there is some convincing evidence that he reached 49° - 50° north latitude, landed on Vancouver Island, and claimed it as the territory of New Albion for his Queen.[1] It was on the authority of Drake's explorations that England claimed original sovereignty over the area that is now British Columbia. England's interest in a new trade route to the Orient was keen, for all of the practicable routes then known, whether by land or by sea, were under the domination of other nations. The infidel Turk and the Mongols sat astride the land routes through Asia Minor. The Spanish and Portuguese controlled the southern sea lanes via Cape Horn and the Cape of Good Hope and tended to block any ship passing that way. England needed a route of her own that would permit her access to the wealth of valuable goods the Orient had to offer.

England's trade with the Far East was chiefly in silk, incense and spices. Of these three, the spice trade was the most important, as few spices were grown in the Western World. Cloves, nutmeg, cinnamon, ginger, and pepper were the most in demand. They were coveted by those who could indulge themselves, not only to flavour their otherwise plain-tasting food, but also as food preservatives in those days when refrigeration was not available and salt, the only alternative, tended to reduce whatever it touched to the lowest denominator of delectability. But the most popular use for spices was as medicines. In every home that could afford one, there was an ornate confection (or comfite) box that doubled as what today would be called a medicine cabinet. The confection box contained different kinds of sugar pastilles made from seeds, spices and herbs mixed with honey and saffron, to be used when therapeutic occasion arose.

Ginger was considered a cure for the even-then prevalent problem of halitosis. It was also considered a stomachic, a digestant, a cure for flatulence, toothache, bleeding gums and as a strengthening agent for loose teeth and weak eyes. Could one ask for more? Sesame seeds soaked in sparrows' eggs and cooked in milk were said to be a potent aphrodisiac; mixed with vinegar and applied to the forehead, they strengthened the brain; blended with crow's gall they served as an embrocation for impotence. Sesame seeds were said to have the additional advantage of allowing a judicious user to open secret passages and hidden caves. Ground-up cinnamon bark was another corrective for bad breath and was also considered a tonic for the heart, liver, kidneys, gall and nerves. It was also a sedative for expectant mothers during childbirth. Cloves, a native of the Molucca (Spice) Islands had similar tonic properties as well as being a preventative for paralysis of the tongue, inflammation of the gums and loosening of the teeth. Rosewater flavoured with cloves was used as an eyewash. Many spices, in addition to their piquant flavour, were and still are reputed to have some hallucinogenic properties. One may ponder their effect on the mind of impressionable man in those days of rampant superstition.

It was the apothecary, the general practitioner of the times, who dispensed the spices. He was skilled in the arts of prescribing and compounding them, having long been a member of the Grocers Company and the Pepperers and Spicers before that. Because of the increasing importance of the new art of compounding medicines, King James in 1617 granted a charter to the Apothecaries that gave them some standing of their own, removing them from the influence of the unskilled Grocers.

To us, the attribution of therapeutic properties to a common cooking aid may serve merely to confirm our low opinion of the state of the medical arts of the time. To those living in the Renaissance, the use of spices as medicines was a welcome step forward, for until then the alternatives were such distinctly less pleasant healing aids as the various species of witches' brew. Spices were undoubtedly refreshing to an odorous unhygienic oral cavity that reeked of carious teeth, pyorrheaic gums and fetid breath. Selected spices also served to titillate the often weary taste buds of that dietically primitive era and tended to soothe some of the postprandial burps and burns, even as the essence of cloves and peppermint is found to do today.

One may gauge the value of the spices to the European economy of the fifteenth and sixteenth centuries by noting that the leader of Magellan's expedition, Juan Sebastian del Cano, who completed the first documented circumnavigation of the globe after Magellan was killed in the Philippine Islands, was honoured by being given a coat of arms that was augmented by two bars of cinnamon, twelve cloves and three nutmegs. Drake, too, paid tribute to the value of these condiments, for not only did he cease his looting of the fabulous Spanish treasure ships to look for the Northwest Passage, but he found room in an already overburdened ship loaded with silver, gold and precious stones for a cargo of spices to carry home to England with him from the Molucca Islands.

A medical man, the Asiatic priest-physician Hoei-Shin, had been the first outsider to reach and influence the Pacific Northwest coast. Now another brand of medicine was to figure in the history of the coast. Europe's clamour for the spices of the Orient, with their fabled medicinal properties, became a major motivating factor in the discovery and charting of the coastline and the establishment of the British influence in British Columbia.

The Stranger Arrives

IN SPITE OF DRAKE'S FAILURE to find the western outlet of a marine passage between the Atlantic and Pacific oceans, rumours of its existence multiplied. They were fed primarily by the apocryphal stories of Juan de Fuca and "Admiral de Fonte."

Juan de Fuca, a Greek working for the Spaniards in California, claimed that, in the year 1512, he had found the western entrance of the fabled passage and described its landmarks and its position. The straits that now bear his name were found by other explorers at the approximate position indicated by him, lending credence to his tale.

Admiral de Fonte was a mythical character invented by one James Petiver (with some assistance, it was said, from Jonathan Swift, author of Gulliver's Travels, and Defoe, creator of Robinson Crusoe). The story was printed complete with chart in the April and June issues of the magazine *Monthly Miscellany or Memoirs for the Curious* in 1708. It was not taken too seriously until, a few years later, a returning seaman claimed to have sailed through de Fonte's passage — and the search was revitalized. To add more zest to the quest, England offered a reward of £20,000 (a fabulous sum when related to the purchasing power of the day) to the discoverer of the waterway.

In the mid eighteenth century, the Spanish became uneasy about the persistent rumours of a Northwest Passage. They were still uncertain as to how Drake had appeared in the Pacific Ocean to loot their ships and they were equally uncertain as to how he had left after doing so. If he had come through a Northwest Passage, others could repeat the journey, and so Juan Perez was sent from California in his ship *Santiago*, for a look at the area.[1] Perez tentatively explored the coast as far north as the Queen Charlotte Islands. Others followed him, and the English became alarmed that the Spanish might not only find the western outlet of the Northwest Passage, but deprive them of their territorial rights, as well.

To forestall the eventuality, Captain James Cook was commissioned in 1776 to sail the two Royal Navy ships *Resolution* and *Discovery* to the Northwest coast and explore and chart the area, with particular reference to the possible existence of any inter-ocean passage. When he failed to find any such passage, Captain George Vancouver, in *Discovery*, and the armed tender *Chatham*, was sent in 1790 to explore and chart whatever had been missed by Cook. While there, he was to meet with the Spanish at Nootka on Vancouver Island and assert England's right to the country.

When Captain Cook's ships returned to England with reports of finding the valuable skins of sea otters, there was a sudden surge of interest in the coast.[2] An increasing number of English, American and Spanish ships sailed for Nootka Sound. But, though some shore bases were established, the white population came, lived and departed in ships until the year 1827, when the land-based Hudson's Bay Company moved northward from Fort Vancouver, near the mouth of the Columbia River, and established permanent trading posts at Fort Langley, Fort Victoria, Fort Mc-Loughlin and Fort Simpson on the coast. The fairness of their trading practices and the permanence of the posts quickly forced the itinerant and often unscrupulous seagoing fur trader out of business. A new white man's era was established that lasted until 1849, when the Hudson's Bay Company handed control of the territories to a duly appointed Governor, representing the British Crown.

A Sailor's Life

IT WAS A TIME OF SHIPS. For the first fifty years after Cook's
arrival at Nootka the white settlers on the coast put down no true
roots. They remained a nautical complement, on loan to the land
from the sea. Sailors and voyagers, they brought to the shore-
side outposts the sailor's ways, the sailor's ailments and the sailor's
cures. Thus, it is nautical life and nautical practice we must consult in order to form a picture of the white man's early medicine
on the coast.

The sea lanes along the coast soon swelled with traffic. As
many as thirty ships could be found anchored at one time at
Friendly Cove, in Nootka Sound. Attracted by rich harvests of
trade, lured by uncharted waterways and unexplored valleys, the
vessels sailed in from England, Boston, California, India and
China. By and large, it was the Englishman who came most often,
and the Englishman who stayed. But a quick glance at Royal
Navy records, with a view toward medical history, will prove
disappointing.

Meticulously detailed logs were kept aboard each ship to record
the happenings of the day. Unfortunately for the medical historian, however, illnesses and injuries among the crew were
deemed of so little consequence that none were mentioned, unless
the working and the safety of the ship was affected. The Royal
Navy did require their surgeons to keep a daily record of illness,

but, after a cursory review, these journals were apparently discarded as not worth keeping.

The extant Royal Naval records of the time do document to some extent the living and working conditions of the sailor. And considerable medical data can be gleaned from some of the extraordinary events chronicled in the available logs of the ships that visited the coast. By interrelating these accounts, it is possible to piece together some of the health problems faced by a seaman afloat off early British Columbia.

A citizen of the twentieth century would be appalled at the prospect of putting up with the discomforts and inconveniences that an ordinary shorebound Englishman of the eighteenth century took for granted. The lot of the British sailor of the time was considerably worse, though his living conditions were mitigated to a certain extent by the anticipation of excitement and adventuring in foreign lands, the sharing in monetary profits following a successful trading venture and even, if very lucky, the possibility of a share in such prize money as the £20,000 offered for the discovery of the Northwest Passage. It was said that a sailor's life was a short but merry one.

Most of the regular sailors in the Royal Navy made competent and decent crews, having been born and bred to the sea as fishermen, or apprenticed from orphanages. In time of war, however, when naval manpower was short, it was a case of any able-bodied man would do, and the prisons and other institutions were drained of debtors, felons and madmen to be made into sailors. If these measures fell short, a captain had the authority to send a squad ashore or aboard merchant vessels to impress needed sailors into the service. This "press gang" was permitted to seize a sailor (a term of increasingly blurred meaning as the war wore on) no matter what he was doing at the time. The waterfront pubs were favourite hunting grounds, but the chase also ranged out into the streets and any healthy-looking fellow, casually walking home with his girl companion, was liable to be whisked away and put aboard ship, not to be seen again by family or friends for many years.

The navy had found by bitter experience that many of the

prospective sailors, whether impressed or volunteer, were so filthy and clothed in such verminous rags that, for the sake of hygiene and sanitation, it was necessary to place them aboard an intermediary vessel for a period of quarantine before assigning them to a man-of-war. After a suitable time, the recruit was given a quick once-over and required to make his mark beside a document that stated, among other disclaimers, " . . . that I have no rupture nor was ever troubled with fits and that I am in no way disabled by lameness or otherwise but have perfect use of my limbs and that I have voluntarily enlisted to serve His Britainnic Majesty King George III. . . . " The tar-to-be was then clothed in a Fearnought Jacket and Trowsers and enrolled as a *bona fide* sailor in the Royal Navy, for which he received eight pence per day and the privilege of being flogged to death or promoted, hanged or rewarded in the name of the King he had sworn to serve. Once a man was aboard a warship he never knew when he would set foot on land again. It might be five or ten years before he was paid off, depending on the needs of God, country or his captain.

On board ship he was given a hammock that contained a straw mattress, familiarly known as a "donkey's breakfast," and two blankets. The hammock was to be slung from the beams and each man was allowed a width of only fourteen inches. Slung side by side across the width of the ship, each slightly overlapped those forward and aft like sardines in a tin. However, with a normal watch system, every alternate hammock would be empty, thus providing more room. The quarters he slept in were poorly heated, when at all, and the shivering fellow had no way of drying himself if he came below wet, other than to climb into his hammock and steam himself dry using his own body heat. The air below decks tended to be foul and, in many parts of the ship, a candle lowered into the hold often as not went out for lack of oxygen. A more "scientific" test used in the men's quarters was the measurement of the length of time it took the foul air to tarnish a silver spoon.

The sailor's diet was carefully regulated, but his rations at best would be considered unappetizing by modern standards. The meat, likely as not, would have been in salt for several years before being eaten, by which time it needed a magician rather than a cook to make it palatable. The salt pork was rather more tolerable than the beef, but sailors were known to carve fancy articles such as boxes out of the beef and the flesh was said to have taken on a good polish not unlike close-grained wood. The ship's biscuits or hardtack came alive with weevils soon after sailing and it was considered prudent to consume these staples in the dark of night to minimize the assault on the eyes by the activities of the biscuit.

Water was stored in casks. It was not purified first and soon became cloudy and smelly from contaminating organisms. Fortunately, as the life cycle of the bacteria progressed, algae intervened and the water cleared again. On long voyages, water was often in short supply and Cook used a still to augment his stores.

If the seaman's intake of nourishment involved certain hardships, the associated outputs called for even greater stoicism. The toilet "facilities" of the officers were fairly good, as they had their night commodes in their cabins and, for daytime use, quarter galleries at the stern of the ship. "Facilities" for the ordinary seaman were far more rugged, hardly conducive to good bowel habits, and constipation was a common problem among sailors. There were urine tubs[1] below decks but, when nature called seriously, he had to go forward to the bow of the ship, climb over the rail and balance himself precariously on the "necessary seat" extending from the beak head, clinging for his life with one hand and hanging on to his trousers with the other as the ship plunged through the waves in a motion that combined with the brush of the flying spray to cleanse both man and vessel of the ensuing pollution. Sir Sheldon Dudley summarized the value of the practice when he said, "the seaman, for generations, has unwittingly observed the fundamental sanitary law of keeping his ingesta apart from his egesta."

To numb his sensitivity, to dull his taste for food, to fire his energy and, in general, to make his life more bearable, an issue was made of a gallon of beer per day per man and, when that ran out, an issue was made twice daily of one half pint of fiery rum or brandy, diluted with water in a mixture called grog.[2] The ameliorating purpose of the alcohol was undoubtedly served but the sailor, human nature being what it is, could not let well enough alone and often saved or traded his rations, with the result that treatment for drunkenness became the most frequent therapeutic problem of the naval surgeon. Another complication of the daily issue was that, as the inebriate weaved his way under the low beams of the betweendecks space, he frequently bumped his head on the obstructing timbers. Head injuries were so common, whether the victim was intoxicated or not, that they were considered an occupational hazard by the sailor and were claimed as a factor in the surprisingly high rate of insanity aboard ship.

It is noteworthy that, in those days of poor treatment for sailors, there was evidence of the beginning of a social security scheme. According to the Act of 1773, two fictitious names per one-hundred complement were listed on the ship's books for wages but not for victuals. The pay accruing to these men, who were called "widowsmen," was to be distributed to the widows of those killed in action. In another charitable effort, the effects of all men who died at sea were auctioned off, with the proceeds going to their families. High prices were customarily paid, in tribute to the worthiness of the cause.

Before death was allowed to claim a stricken seaman, however, the forces of medicine were called upon to intervene, in the person of the sea surgeon. This gentleman often was a conscientious and humane practitioner. His qualifications, unfortunately, could at best be considered marginal, even in those medically marginal times. In eighteenth-century England, the practice of medicine was carried on by the physicians ("prescribers of the physic") and chirurgeons who held a doctorate in medicine, the drug-dispensing apothecary, here and there a practical nurse — and the surgeon, certified as such by the Company of Barber Surgeons. The Barber Surgeons were expected to supply surgeons to the navy as part of their charter.

Needless to say, the College of Physicians considered the Barber Surgeons as distinctly inferior types and refused to assist them, even though the surgeon had to act as physician when aboard

57

ship. This uncooperative attitude of the physicians persisted after the dissolution of the Company of Barber Surgeons in 1745 and the formation of the Company of Surgeons, in an attempt to improve the surgeon's standards. It did harm not only to the naval medical service but to the College of Physicians itself and to the advance of health care, in general. Valuable observations of medical problems among seamen often were recorded, but these could not penetrate the barrier of the authoritative conservatism that surrounded the physicians, and many potential discoveries were missed. The observation by a sea captain, in 1752, that malaria and mosquito bites were associated was ignored, as was a scurvy-free voyage to India by Sir Richard Hawkins in 1593, over a century and one-half before Cook's highly acclaimed scurvy-free voyage to the South Pacific.[3]

In the early part of the eighteenth century, a surgeon was certified as such for the navy by the Court of Examiners of the Company of Barber Surgeons after a fifteen-minute examination that included the time to collect a five-shilling fee.[4] Evidence of dissatisfaction among the fraternity is revealed in the report of a naval surgeon who was captured by the French after an engagement and placed in prison along with the common sailors. He stated that the French, after examining his credentials did not know whether he was a medical man or a barber.

As the century wore on, the sea surgeon acquired better credentials. He could qualify, for example, by taking an undergraduate course in surgery at a university, as did Archibald Menzies,[5] Vancouver's surgeon aboard the *Discovery*. Menzies was interested in botany and attended the University of Edinburgh. While there he also took a course in surgery and it might be said that he majored in botany and minored in surgery. Years later, after his experiences as surgeon with Captain Colnett and later with Captain Vancouver, he received an M.D. from the University of Aberdeen. If a surgeon did not attend university, he could be approved after suitable experience, as was David Samwell. He had served as surgeon's mate under William Anderson on the *Resolution* and, recognizing that experience, Cook appointed him surgeon on the *Discovery* in the shuffle following the death of Anderson.

The training of a surgeon remained for some time rudimentary. He was taught or acquired the principles of amputations of limbs, as that would be his most common operation. Any traumatizing wound of an extremity was considered sufficient indication for lopping off the offended member; the fatal onset of gas gangrene, lockjaw, or other septic condition must be averted at any cost. Pope reports that after one naval action there were sixteen amputations. There were two survivals. Bleeding vessels were ligated with non-absorbable sutures that were left long so that they could be pulled out when they had served their purpose and were sloughed free. The surgeon was taught the difference between the various types of purulent discharges from wounds; he learned to recognize those known as "laudable pus" as being less virulent and a probable precursor of satisfactory healing. The secondary hemorrhage resulting from the infected necrosis of a large vessel called for a negative prognosis; even if the vessel were re-ligated, the sepsis would erode the vessel again and again with all too often a fatal outcome. He was taught that penetrating wounds of the chest and abdomen were hopeless; he was not to waste his time on such cases.

Severe bleeding that could not be controlled by pressure bandages or ligation of a vessel was said to be controlled by the drawing of blood from other parts of the body through venesection to lessen the volume of blood in the bleeding area. Bleeding by venesection was also considered beneficial in severe fevers and other illnesses. Flash burns during action were common, as a result of the spillage of gunpowder during the process of ramming powder and shot down the muzzle of the cannon. The treatment was varied and consisted chiefly of applications of linseed oil, olive oil, or compresses of vinegar. It was taught that vesication and other secondary disturbances could be greatly reduced by the application of ice or ice water to the burned area.

The surgeon wore no uniform aboard ship. He was designated a "Warrant Officer of Wardroom Rank," along with the Purser and the ship's Master, and was thus distinguished from the Boatswain, Gunner and Carpenter.[6] He was considered a craftsman and ranked below the Master of the ship and above his fellow

Insignia of the Sea Surgeon.

civilian, the Purser. The surgeon's pay amounted to five pounds per month. Although he was not a doctor of medicine, aboard ship he was expected to assume the physician's role and to treat the fluxes, fevers and other afflictions of the sailor as best he could. Neither was he an apothecary, but he soon learned to make the pills and mix the potions of the limited pharmacopœia then available. He was to keep a daily record of all illnesses and injury in the form of a Journal of Practice and this was to be turned in to the Naval Sick and Hurt Board at the end of the voyage. He was to visit the sick twice a day and present a sick list to the captain daily. If a sailor was too ill to work, he was relieved of his duties and given a Certificate of Illness to show the officer commanding the watch.

When a surgeon signed aboard a man-of-war, his chief responsibility was to those injured in naval actions. Although the explorers' ships were armed with cannon, just in case, they did not normally engage in heavy action. Often, they carried letters of protection from French, Spanish, Dutch and American authorities that allowed them to proceed on their highly respected scientific missions unmolested even in the event of war. In consequence, their surgeons found the time to take an active interest in many non-medical activities.

Anderson of the *Resolution* was a linguist, botanist and naturalist.

John MacKay, surgeon on Captain James Strange's vessels, was a naturalist and botanist who, after successfully treating Chief Maquinna's daughter for a skin lesion, decided to stay and study the flora and fauna of the country.[7] He landed at Friendly Cove complete with livestock, seeds for a garden and other supplies to become what might be termed the first white settler in B.C. Fourteen months later, after losing all of his supplies and equipment and having had to live like an Indian for many months, he seemed glad to be picked up by the *Imperial Eagle*, a trading ship of Austrian registry, on its arrival at Nootka. It was his report that Nootka was on an island that led eventually to Captain Vancouver's voyage to circumnavigate that island and search behind it for a possible opening of the Northwest Passage.

Vancouver's Archibald Menzies was another botanist surgeon and his studies of the flora of the British Columbia coast became world famous. His was the original description of the beautiful arbutus tree that is found so plentifully on the rocky shore and it was named after him — *Arbutus Menzii*.

It may be mentioned that, as botanists and naturalists, the surgeons finally were found to be worthy of a uniform and quarter-deck rank. It was a distinction they could never have achieved as mere surgeons.

Perhaps the most outstanding example of the sea surgeon who subordinated his medical training to other scientific interests was the Spaniard José Mariano Moziño — the botanist-naturalist of the Royal Scientific Expedition to the "Northern limits of California" under Bogeda y Quadra.[8] He arrived at Nootka in 1792 and later wrote a classic report on Nootka and its inhabitants. Moziño is of particular interest, as he was not only the first fully qualified physician to come to Nootka, but he arrived with a degree taken at a medical school on the North American continent. Although he undoubtedly gave medical help when it was needed, the evidence indicates that he did not pursue a medical career after receiving his Bachelor of Medicine degree from the Royal and Pontifical University of Mexico in 1787. He apparently had an inquisitive mind and while at the university acquired degrees in philosophy, theology and ethics as well as in botany and, in addition, gained sufficient knowledge to be able to substitute for a time in the Chair of Astrology and Mathematics. With such an educational background, it is understandable, perhaps, that his active mind found more to occupy it in the expanding worlds of botany and natural history than in the dormant world of medicine.

The function of the ship's surgeon in looking after the medical problems aboard was clear. Less clear, but at least equal in importance, was the role of the captain. The one person who assumes responsibility for all things that take place on his ship, including the health of its men, is the officer commanding. It was and is his prerogative, among other things, to set rules and regulations that he believed would ensure a healthy crew. It was most important to him that his men were in the best of condition in those days of sail, as the sailors supplied the vital manpower that was the sole means of trimming the sails and handling the ship during fair weather and foul, whether in the turbulent latitudes of the roaring forties or the more peaceful ones of the benevolent trade winds. Crew replacements in distant lands were few and far between. Preventative medicine had to be practised in the fields of hygiene and nutrition, the only fields, apart from surgery, that yielded any beneficial results. It was thus the responsibility of a layman, the captain, to prevent illness by making and enforcing regulations that ensured proper sanitation, hygiene and an adequate nutritional diet. The representative of the medical profession, the ship's surgeon, was left to his menial tasks as a hewer of limbs and a drawer of blood. The captain attended to higher matters.

Captain Cook was one of the first commanders to assume effective responsibility for the health of his crew. As a result of his efforts, Cook was given the Royal Society's Copley Medal when he returned from his first voyage of exploration to Australia and the southern seas. He had completed the long voyage without the loss of a single man from scurvy. His success was a direct result of his strictly enforced dietary, hygienic and sanitary measures. Vancouver, who had served under Cook as a midshipman, was able to profit by Cook's experiences and to do even better than his mentor. On his four-and-one-half-year voyage, the *Discovery* lost six men: one died of disease, one was poisoned, one was an apparent suicide and three were lost through accident. The *Chatham* did not lose a man. Vancouver's mortality rate at sea was one-third the normal rate in England. On Cook's voyage to the Pacific Northwest, the *Resolution* lost three sailors through illness and four marines — plus the good captain himself — who were killed. The *Discovery* had no deaths.

THERE WERE UNDOUBTEDLY A GREAT NUMBER of sick sailors on
and off the coast during those early days. As many sicknesses and
injuries tended to be shrugged off as commonplace and inevitable,
few records have survived that relate their case histories. Others
have been more adequately documented. One of the latter is
scurvy.

This disease was dreaded and feared by all sailors — with good
reason. Its effects were horrible to witness and lethal in consequence once it appeared aboard ship. The symptoms of the
disease are described, in part, by Lussads, writing about the effects
of scurvy among the crews of Vasco da Gama's ships on the
voyages to India in 1496.[1]

> A dread disease in rankling horrors shed
> and deaths dire ravage through mine army spread
> never mine eyes such dreary sight beheld
> ghastly the mouths and gums enormous swelling
> and instant, putrid like a dead man's wound
> poisoned with fetid streams the air around
> no sage physicians ever watchful zeal
> no skillful surgeons gentle hand to heal
> were found; each weary mournful hour we gave
> some brave companion to a foreign grave.

A classic example of the havoc scurvy could wreak is illustrated
in the tragic outcome of the English globe-circling expedition

under Commodore Anson in 1740-44. Seven ships proudly sailed from England. Only one returned. Of the 1,955 men aboard when they set off, 1,051 died, mostly from scurvy. As all the survivors, as well, had suffered from scurvy during the voyage, the ships were not only undermanned, but staffed with crews so debilitated that they were unable to keep their vessels under control, leading to the loss of six of the seven ships.

In spite of Cook's precedent-setting example of how to run a scurvy-free ship, the logs of several ships reported an incidence of scurvy on arrival in the Pacific Northwest. Strange, in command of the trading ships *Captain Cook* and *The Experiment*, landed his scorbutic sailors at Nootka to speed their recovery. Captain Colnett of the *Prince of Wales*, with Menzies aboard as surgeon, recorded that on his arrival at Nootka his crew was so weak from scurvy that the Indians had to help them ashore. Captain Dixon of the *King George* and Captain Portlock of the *Queen Charlotte* had similar problems. Captain Meares in the *Nootka* lost 23 men.

Scurvy first became a problem at sea during the tenth and eleventh centuries, when sails replaced oars as a means of propelling ships. The sails enabled the ships to remain away from land far longer than oar-power. Longer absences from land meant longer periods of dependence on grossly inadequate diets, thus opening the door to deficiency disease.

Scurvy is a disease caused by a shortage of Vitamin C. The human body is unable to store the vitamin in large quantities; as a consequence, a low Vitamin-C diet quickly brings on a deficiency state. As vitamins and their significance were not known in those days, the true etiology was not suspected. It had been observed that the condition was associated with the restricted diet aboard ship and could be cured by eating fresh foods. Fresh foods were largely unavailable on long voyages, and no other method of prevention was understood. For that reason, Cook's scurvy-free voyages were heralded as epoch-making. Cook attributed his good results to the sanitary, hygienic and dietary regime he enforced aboard his ships. The betweendecks area was kept clean and as dry as possible by airing the ship well in good weather and, in bad weather, using portable fires. Gunpowder mixed with vinegar was burned to counteract obnoxious vapours from the bilges and other places. To conserve the strength of his sailors, he divided them into three watches. To keep them clean and healthy, the officers saw to it that their hammocks, their clothes and themselves were well aired and washed. A condensed preparation called portable soup along with sauerkraut were relied on as dietary supplements and were considered an integral part of the anti-scorbutic regime. Malt in the form of beer was considered by many to be a powerful anti-scorbutic, but Cook was not impressed by its effects. He relied rather on fresh water whenever he could get it and eked his supplies out by using a still made of copper tubing and old musket barrels. He made vigorous efforts to obtain greens of any variety and flavour whenever he landed and one of his lieutenants, a man by the name of Home wrote, "It was his practice to cause great quantities of green stuff to be boiled amongst the pease, soup and wheat and cared not much whether they were bitter or sweet, so as he was but certain they had no pernicious quality and frequently to one who considered only the pleasing of the taste without having respect to health the messes were somewhat spoiled but as there was nothing else to be got they were obleedged to eat them and it was no uncommon thing that when swallowing over these mess(es) to curse him heartily and wish for God's sake that he might be obleedged to eat such damned stuff mixed with his broth as long as he lived. Yet for all that there were none so ignorant as not to know how right a thing it was." Apparently, Cook made at least one mistake, having dug up some roots that he thought were similar to carrots. Those that ate them became violently ill. Home suggests that they might have been hemlock roots.[2]

Cook's efforts to ensure an adequate diet often took both psychology and disciplinary action. Shortly after leaving England for the Pacific Northwest, two of his crew members refused to eat fresh meat, while it was still available. Cook solved the problem in a seaman-like manner by giving the two a dose of the cat-o'-nine-tails. There was no more of that trouble throughout the rest of the voyage. Cook relied greatly on sauerkraut as an anti-scorbutic food — a lesson he had learned from the Dutch.

The sailors balked at eating it and the wily Cook withdrew their rations of the stuff and had it served instead at the officers' mess, where it was eaten with inspired gusto. The desired reaction soon set in and the men began to grumble about the officers eating their sauerkraut. Cook restored their rations and the men discovered that they had miraculously acquired a taste for their 'kraut.

Captain Vancouver had sailed with Cook and learned his lessons well. His voyage was longer than any of Cook's, covering a period of four and a half years, with only one serious outbreak of scurvy. Vancouver was mystified as to the cause of the outbreak, but the puzzle was solved when the cook voluntarily confessed that he had been coerced by certain members of the crew into breaking the dietary rules established by the captain. The fact that Vancouver forgave the cook and did not use the lash on him was quoted as an example of Vancouver's sense of justice and fair play.

The daily ration of one gallon of beer per day per man was regarded as a pleasant anti-scorbutic. When a ship's supply of beer ran out, as it frequently did, a party of men was sent ashore to make what was called spruce beer.[3] This was made by boiling the small branches of spruce or other evergreens for several hours in a large cauldron and then adding molasses, water and a fermenting agent, such as yeast or wort. After straining, it was put in a cask to work, and contemporary writers praise the resultant brew's flavour and potable quality.

In the increasingly active and powerful Royal Navy of the late 18th century, the effects of scurvy were more of a handicap than the damage inflicted by the enemy. Thus, the scurvy-free voyages of Cook and Vancouver were welcomed as the first breakthrough in the campaign against the disease. Unfortunately, these shipboard victories were obtained by the establishment and enforcement of complex health regimes that depended for their success on the strict attention to a multiplicity of details by unusually competent captains.

Such regimes were difficult to duplicate. And, ironically, the very interest created by their success actually retarded the final solution to the problem of scurvy for many years. In 1747, twenty years before Cook's first scurvy-free voyage to Australia, Dr. James Lind had demonstrated in controlled experiments the value of lemon juice as a prophylactic against scurvy. As so often happens when a physician tries to "sell" his discovery to the layman, the true worth of his work was not accepted. There were some in the navy who had an inkling of the power of the sour fruit. Both Cook and Vancouver were given supplies of concentrated lemon juice to test as a cure, should scurvy break out. It was not used, and nothing was proved. It was not until 1793 that the prophylactic use of lemon juice was tested on the Mediterranean Fleet and proved so successful that a regime of daily issues was instituted in 1795 throughout the rest of the fleet.

The conquest of scurvy came at an opportune time. The acid cure scored against more than just a disease, for it apparently curdled the sweet career of one Napoleon Bonaparte. The absence of scurvy enabled Admiral Nelson to keep his ships at sea for long periods and effectively blockade the seaports of France. This led inexorably to the downfall of the Corsican.

13

Sex and the Seaman

LOVE MAKES THE HEAD SPIN and the world go round. The mingling of the genes and chromosomes of unrelated individuals keeps human evolution on course. Perverse nature, in need of a fuel to keep the evolutionary pot bubbling, created sexual desire, made it into a powerful force — and then apparently decided she'd made it *too* powerful. To control the potent gene-disseminating force that she'd unleashed, she hit upon the device of fear. Lover, take care! Yonder lies the danger of fearful suffering and disgrace!

Venereal disease is well understood today. The main types have been identified as syphilis and gonorrhea, with an occasional admixture of chancroid. Public awareness of these diseases, the growth of tolerance and the effectiveness of antibiotics have combined to initiate some measure of relief and control.

In the eighteenth century, the venereal diseases were not well distinguished from one another and there was no control. Gonorrhea, chancroid and yaws (an ulcerating disease caused by a spirochete similar to that of syphilis) were more or less lumped together, with syphilis — the grand pox — being blamed for most of them. Treatment was a dismal prospect, rarely worth the attendant humiliations. It ranged from the usual nostrums and purges to inunctions of mercury that had some effect, though only when used early and correctly.

The sexual life of the eighteenth-century sailor did little to help matters. The meeting of his needs could at best be described as an uneven affair. At sea, no women were on hand to quiet his clamor. In port, he was not allowed ashore for fear he would desert the ship. To satisfy his wants when his vessel arrived in harbour, boat loads of prostitutes were ferried out to the ship by local entrepreneurs. When the ship had been secured, the waterman was given permission to bring his boat alongside and the sailors descended on its cargo. Each eventually picked his partner, paying the boatman a shilling or so for her passage. The scene betweendecks must have possessed a certain Hogarthian splendour, with its men and women crowded together in a confined space with no thought to privacy, hygiene, sanitation, or modesty. The filth and stench must have outrivalled that ascribed to the Indians at Nootka. These and the attendant blasphemy, drunkenness, quarrels, riots and fighting turned the ship into "a hell afloat."

One need scarcely wonder that venereal disease was so commonplace among sailors as to be considered an occupational ailment. If the sufferer reported to the surgeon for relief, he was fined, deprived of his daily issue of spirits and any liberty he had coming and sent back to his duties. As a result, most sailors hid their affliction as best they could and, gradually, it became chronic. Those who did report to the surgeon were usually in great distress from such complications as urinary retention, paraphimosis, and epididymitis. Chronic or acute, the disease remained transmissible.

There are no archaeological findings that would indicate venereal disease was extant in British Columbia before the white man came but there are records of its presence among the natives soon afterwards.[1] The question of who introduced it among the Indians — the English from Europe, the Spaniards from the south, or the Russians from the north — has vexed researchers for many years. The following evidence seems to lay the onus squarely on the poor sailors of England.

Captain Cook was well aware of the tragic and often fatal consequences of introducing venereal disease among previously uncontaminated natives. His experiences with the effects of the pox introduced to natives of the Society Islands by his men on a previous visit had caused him great concern. Although he had not allowed any known V.D. carrier ashore, the natives had become infected.

Cook was a remarkably astute medical observer. He recorded his belief that venereal disease could be carried by men who were apparently cured:[2]

It is also a doubt with me that the most skilful of the faculty can tell whether every man who has had the disease is so far cured so as not to communicate it further. I think I could mention some instance on the contrary.

In Hawaii, he posted the following orders in an attempt to control the disease:[3]

... it is therefore Ordered that no Officer or other person (not sent on duty) shall carry with him out of the Ships, or into the Country, any fire Arms whatever, and great care is to be taken to keep the Natives ignorant of the method of charging such as we may be under a necessity to make use of. And whereas there are Venereal complaints remaining onboard the Ships, and in order to prevent as much as possible the communicating this fatal disease to a set of innocent people, it is hereby ordered that no Woman on any pretence whatever be admitted onboard the Resolution without my permission, nor onboard the Discovery but by permission of Captain Clerke. And whoever brings a woman into the Ships, or suffers her to come in of her own accord contrary to this Order shall be punished; and if any person having, or suspected of having the Venereal disease or any Symptoms thereof, shall lie with any Woman, he shall also be severely punished, and no such suspected persons (of whom a List is to be kept on the Quarter Deck) shall be suffered to go onshore on any pretence whatever. Given under my hand Onboard His Majesty's Sloop the Resolution at Sea this 26th of November 1778. Jams Cook.

In spite of these orders, one William Bradley found the charms of the native women so irresistible that he was obliged to receive two dozen lashes for "disobeying orders and having connections with women knowing himself to have the Venereal Disorder on him."

It would hardly seem reasonable to propose that Cook subsequently arrived at Nootka with crews composed exclusively of healthy, uninfected males. That the sailors enjoyed intercourse with the Indian women is authenticated in the following extract from Samwell's log, written with his customary wit and vigour: [4]

Hitherto we had seen none of their young Women tho' we had often given the men to understand how agreeable their Company would be to us & how profitable to themselves, in consequence of which they about this time brought two or three Girls to the Ships: tho' some of them had faces yet as they were exceedingly dirty their Persons at first sight were not very inviting, however our young Gentlemen were not to be discouraged by such an obstacle as this which they found was to be removed with Soap and warm water, this they called the Ceremony of Purification and were themselves the Officiators at it, & it must be mentioned to their praise that they performed it with much piety & Devotion, taking as much pleasure in cleansing a naked young Woman from all Impurities in a Tub of Warm Water, as a young Confessor would absolve a beautiful Virgin who was about to sacrifice that Name to himself. This Ceremony appeared very strange to the Girls, who in order to render themselves agreeable to us had taken particular pains to daub their Hair and faces well with red oaker which to their great astonishment we took as much pains to wash off. Such are the different Ideas formed by different nations of Beauty and cleanliness: they were prevailed upon to sleep on board the Ships, or rather forced to it by their Fathers or other Relations who brought them on board. In their behaviour they were very modest and timid, in which they differed very much from the South Sea Island Girls who in general are impudent and loud.

Their Fathers who generally accompanied them made the Bargain & received the price of the Prostitution of their Daughters, which was commonly a Pewter plate well scoured for one night. When they found that this was a profitable Trade they brought more young women to the Ships, who in compliance with our prepostorous Humor spared themselves the trouble of laying on their Paint and us of washing it off again by making themselves tolerable clean before they came to us, by which they found they were more welcome Visitors and thus by falling in with our ridiculour Notions (for such no doubt they deemed them) they found means at last to disburthen our young Gentry of their Kitchen furniture, many of us after leaving this Harbour not being able to muster a plate to eat our Salt beef from. But as we found the following Maxim, 'No Bankrupt ever found a fair one kind,' hold true in this part of the Globe, & had been stripped of all our Hatchets & iron trade by the beautiful Nymphs of the South Sea Islands, we were reduced to the Dilemma of parting with these Articles or of renouncing all Claim to the favour of these fair Americans, & it may well be supposed that we chose the better part, that we enjoyed the present Day & left the Morrow to provide for itself — and to provide tables and chests to eat our Salt Beef and pork from instead of plates.

Another extract from Samwell's descriptive log seems to dispose of the Spaniards and Russians as possible sources of the grand pox. The occasional Catholic backslider must not be ruled out, but neither should such rare lapses be considered a major source of infection. Samwell records:[5]

Monday, October 24, 1778: — The Russians have been obliged to use harsh Methods to bring the Natives of Nawanalaska & the other Islands into subjection & to make them honest. They told us they never forgave a Theft but always punished it with instant death. They always expressed their disapprobation of our intercourse with the Indian Women, and with a very grave Phyz seemed to lament our depravity in having Connection with those who they said were 'neet Christaine', that is not Christians, and it is probable that this Circumstance may restrain these godly People from meddling with any other Furr in these regions than that of the Sea Beaver. This would, notwithstanding their remonstrances, have appeared impossible to us had we not met with an instance of the like before. We were told of the beautiful Nymphs of Otaheite immediately on our arrival at that Island, that the Spaniards during their Abode among them would have nothing to say to them, even those good natured Creatures were so obliging as to make their first Advances & come in their Canoes along side their ships, they were never suffered to go on board. This appeared very strange to these blooming Girls, who had always been so eagerly courted by us, & who could have no Idea of any defect that would render young Women undesirable Objects except the Want of Personal Charms; female Pride, the conscious Dignity of Beauty, were most sensibly touched by this outrageous insult & they frequently complained to us of this unmanly Behaviour of the flesh subduing Dons. We gave them every consolation in our power. Where the Hand of Nature has lavishly adorned the Form of a fair Damsel & spread the bewitching bloom of beauty o'er her lovely face — blind sinners that we are — we could never yet perceive the Want of the Finger of the Priest to mark her Forehead with the Sign of the Cross — .

So it would appear that the Englishman at Nootka not only bestowed on the Indians the blessing of his genes, the effect of which could be predicted to last virtually forever, but also an affliction that could disrupt health "even onto the third and fourth generation."

The labyrinthine ways of venereal disease are illustrated in the case of an officer who died in November of 1789 as a result of what would appear to be a long-standing illness that was a common complication of gonorrhea. Although he died in Canton, his illness was undoubtedly active while sailing off the Northwest coast. He was William MacLeod, first mate on the *King George*, and the following entry in the log of the companion ship *Queen Charlotte*, as written by Captain Driver, tells the story. Both ships had been trading along the coast — the Queen Charlotte Islands had been named after Captain Driver's vessel — and they were now in Canton to sell their furs. Notes Captain Driver:

On the 29th., at three in the afternoon, Mr. William MacLeod, first mate of the *King George*, departed this life. His death was not occasioned by any disorder caught during the present voyage but from an old complaint in the urethra which frequently occasioned a suppression of urine and other alarming symptoms, during the latter part of the voyage. At the time of his being taken ill (which was on the 28th) he was on a visit on board Locko Indiaman, and his drinking some stale porter after dinner brought on so violent a relapse of his disorder, as was supposed to be the immediate cause of his death. He died universally lamented by his friends and acquaintances and was interred on the fornoon of the 30th., on Frenchmans Island.[6]

A modern internist might assess the symptoms that afflicted poor MacLeod as indicating a stricture of the urethra, probably gonorrheal in origin, with chronic urinary retention, secondary cystitis and ascending hydronephrosis with pyelonephritis, and renal damage, culminating in acute renal failure, with this last more likely to have been triggered by a general over-indulgence in food and drink during his visit aboard the *Indiaman* than by staleness of the porter itself.

Miscellaneous Afflictions

SMALLPOX WAS A DISEASE SO WIDESPREAD in Europe during the latter part of the eighteenth century that few sailors of the time did not bear its scars. It was called smallpox to distinguish it from the "grand" variety assigned to syphilis. Although the Chinese had instituted a form of prophylactic vaccination as early as the 11th century, Europeans did not have any such protection until Jenner published his experiments with cow-pox vaccination in 1798.

The Indians of the coast had not been exposed to the disease before the white man came and they were very susceptible, as they had no natural immunity. When the Vancouver expedition arrived, it found that the disease had preceded it. Peter Puget, writing in the log of the *Discovery* in August of 1792, states in reference to the Indians in the Queen Charlotte-Fitzhugh Sound area:

> The small pox most have had and most terribly pitted they are indeed many have lost their eyes and no doubt it has raged with, uncommon severity amongst them —

So it would seem that the white man wasted no time in introducing not only the grand pox, but also the small. Epidemics of the latter recurred among the Indians over the next hundred years, one of the most severe breaking out in the Queen Charlotte Islands in 1795.

In 1862, it was reported that smallpox left only 15 Indians alive out of an original band of 800 in the Bella Coola area. Such devastating epidemics created a deep resentment among the Indians, who understood that the white man was to blame.[1] This resentment was one of the reasons given for the massacre of a white road crew in Bute Inlet in 1865.

Just who was responsible for the introduction of smallpox to the Pacific Northwest is difficult to determine with certainty. Most of the ships that came to the coast had been long at sea. They were staffed with men whose faces were marked by the healed scars of the pox pustules. These indicated not only immunity for their bearers but safety for those with whom they came in contact. Evidence in the log of Cook's *Resolution* points to Russian traders in Alaska as the possible source of the infection. The Russians had arrived there in 1741, thirty seven years before Cook. When, after Cook's death, Clerke took *Resolution* and *Discovery* to Kamchatka on the Asiatic coast, he wondered at the many Indian villages he found abandoned. The Russians told him that more than 10,000 Indians had died in an epidemic of smallpox introduced from Siberia in 1769. It would seem possible, even probable, that the scourge was communicated from Kamchatka to Alaska by the Russian traders, and that from there it worked its way down the coast to the areas reported by Puget.

Shellfish poisoning was a hazard the coast introduced to the Englishman — rather than vice versa. Vancouver lost one man and had several temporarily afflicted by the neurotoxic poison present in shellfish that had been ingesting planktonic dinoflagellate protozoa.[2] The poison remains a threat to modern-day shellfish eaters in British Columbia. When the dread protozoa appear, the Provincial government puts up signs warning of the potential danger. The toxin-containing protozoa stain the water red over large areas and are known widely as the "Red Tide." The shellfish take in the protozoa as food and are not themselves affected by the poison. Humans eating the shellfish, however, are soon seized with a progressive nerve paralysis that can eventually knock out the vital functions of the body. The degree of paralysis reached depends upon the amount of toxin ingested. Provided it does not attain a lethal level, the action reverses and the patient rapidly recovers. The poisoning of Vancouver's sailors occurred as one of his small boats was charting Finlayson Channel while still searching for the elusive Northwest Passage. The incident is described in the muster book of *HMS Discovery*:[3]

On the 15th June (1792) last, in the latitude of about 52 degrees, thirty minutes, longtitude 230 degrees, both crews experienced a malady which nearly proved fatal to the whole and was attributed to some muscles they had eaten, which were of that pernicious quality as very shortly to affect all those who had eaten of them with a numbness, first in their extremities and then over the whole body, attended with a dizziness in their head; this, however, did not prevent their executing their duty, and the whole of the boats crew pulled their oars, in rowing along shore, near three hours after they had eaten these muscles; but on boats landing, about noon, the instant they left off rowing, three of them were seized in such a manner as to be obliged to be carried out of the boat, when John Carter almost instantly expired; the others not feeling this very subtill poison in so violent a degree as the unfortunate man who lost his life by it. The other men recovered by drinking hot salt water as an emetic but such was their foolish obstinancy that it was not until poor Carter resigned his life that they could be prevailed upon to drink the hot water. His fate however induced them to follow the advice of their officers and the desired effect was produced.

The place where the mussels were eaten was called Poison Cove and the inlet leading to it was named Mussel Inlet. The small bay along Finlayson Arm where Carter was finally buried was named Carter Bay. The names commemorate, among other things, the first recorded case history written on the coast, complete with the complaints of the patient, the etiology of the disease, the diagnosis, the treatment and, at least in one instance, the rather final conclusion.

The bible has supplied us with one of the earliest records of another sailor's affliction. We speak of "the patience of Job," referring to a long-suffering character who was covered with boils, enduring them stoically over a long period of time. Apparently, from the relatively frequent references in the log of the *Chatham*, Lieutenant Puget, now transferred to that ship, was finding his own patience tried by an epidemic of boils among his crew. At first he thought the boils were the result of a change in diet from fresh food to shipboard rations, after having wintered in the Hawaiian Islands. On arrival at Nootka, so many of the crew were ill with generalized furunculosis that help had to be obtained from the Spanish to assist in the careening of the *Chatham* and in the repair of some damaged copper sheating on her bottom.

To Puget's mortification, his sick list at Nootka lengthened, in spite of "the excellence of the refreshments the Cove (Friendly) afforded." The ship was washed and ventilated and fresh fish and venison were added to the daily diet. A batch of spruce beer was made, and Puget "had great hopes from the spruce beer if we could get it to work." Unfortunately, all efforts to make it palatable failed, and its curative potential could not be put to the test. All these nutritional and hygienic activities did little to assuage the activities of the furunculogenic staphylococcus and, over the next many weeks, patient references recur to its continued disabling presence among the crew.[4] Perhaps it gradually died out. Perhaps Puget tired of the repetitious entries. Either way, all mention of boils eventually ceased.

A less transitory and more tragic problem was presented by tuberculosis. Several of the officers aboard the explorers' ships suffered and died from chronic debilitating illnesses that have been presumed to be tuberculosis. Anderson, the surgeon on Cook's *Resolution* and Charles Clerke, a senior officer on the same ship, were both aware of their sickness and its hazards. When Cook was turning north at Tahiti, they asked to be allowed to remain, for they realized they were unlikely to survive the rigours of a long northern voyage. They procrastinated, however, and when their last opportunity to leave the ship came at Hawaii, they were unable to land, for the natives were showing signs of hostility. The two officers were forced to continue north with the ship, and Anderson died off the coast of Alaska. Clerke succumbed somewhat later, after having taken over command of the expedition when Captain Cook was murdered in the Hawaiian Islands. King, who took over command after the death of Clerke, himself died only a few years later of consumption.

Captain Vancouver similarly was suffering from a debilitating illness when he set out on his voyage. Menzies "treated" him from the outset, even though at the beginning Menzies was rated as a "botanist." Vancouver's illness progressed to the point that, on the return voyage, he was so severely handicapped and weak that he was unable to go ashore while putting in at the Cocos Islands. On his return to England, he completed his lengthy reports and died at the Star & Garter Inn at Richmond two years and eight months later, at the age of forty. It has been suggested that he died of Graves disease, commonly known as exophthalmic goitre, but the evidence seems weak in the light of present day knowledge. Tuberculosis has generally been credited as the cause of Vancouver's death.

Adding to the problems of shipboard health were the rats. To modern medical officers, the presence of rats means the possibility of infection. Aboard the old wooden ships rats seemed to thrive in staggering numbers. One Thomas Swaine of Greenwich, styling himself "Rat Catcher to His Majesty's Navy," used white arsenic as a poison bait. On one ship alone he accounted for 2,475 of the rodents. The rats would gnaw their way into the containers holding ship's provisions, leaving their calling cards in the form of little dark infected turds. They were vermin that supported smaller vermin on their bodies and these were potential carriers of typhus, a disease so common aboard ship that it was sometimes known as ship's fever. The rats were apparently so prolific aboard the explorers' ships that they at times were used as an additional source of fresh meat. It is recorded in the log of Cook's last voyage that, when landfall on the west coast of America was made, it was celebrated by "the gentlemen of the gun room dining on a fricasse of rat." These animals, fortunately, were brown rats that had invaded Europe and were gradually killing off the black rats, which had spread the bubonic plague. There seems little doubt that it was the early explorers who achieved the distinction of introducing rats to British Columbia. Moziño noted at Nootka in 1792:[5] "Our ships have carried a colony of rats to these uncivilized countries and these having multiplied prodigiously cause serious damage to the houses of our settlement."

The explorers may have earned the further honour of conveying the ubiquitous cockroach to the New World, for their ships were heavily infested with these passengers, as well. King writes that they were present aboard the *Resolution* and, although they had killed "prodigious numbers" of the insects, these efforts had little apparent effect.

Smaller hurts were sometimes recorded alongside the large. It is noted that one John Turner, seaman, had his right arm fractured on August 7th, 1792. Vancouver's *Discovery* had gone hard aground on the Walker group of rocks in the Queen Charlotte Sound, with a falling tide. The ship was in great danger of being lost and was lightened of all movable gear, including her topmasts. The danger was over and the masts were being replaced when "in swinging up the main topgallant mast the top rope broke, by which means John Turner, seaman, had his right arm fractured." As there is no further information, it is presumed that Turner had his arm "bound in the natural position with a splint and calico compresses," as was the custom of the time.

In 1799, Surgeon A. P. Cranstoun of Vancouver's *Discovery*, along with Mr. Horne, boatswain, were invalided home from Nootka aboard the supply ship *Daedulus*. Cranstoun apparently had been taken seriously ill during an epidemic of the "Flux" (amoebic dysentery, perhaps) contracted from a Dutch ship at Capetown. Archibald Menzies, botanist, was appointed surgeon in his place.

That alcohol was a problem at Nootka was recognized in the log of the *Chatham*. Peter Puget on May 2, 1793, noted that some of the sailors had saved their liquor rations and, apparently, traded or sold them to sailors from the Spanish ship *Princessa*. Two of these got drunk and one was stabbed. A reward of thirty dollars was offered to find out who had sold the liquor, but the money was never collected. The liquor on the *Chatham* was then diluted with five parts of water instead of the usual one part as had been recommended by "Admiral Grog," and it had to be drunk at the tub when dispensed, any balance remaining to be thrown overboard. It was further recorded that some American traders, "Boston men" as they were called, were selling whiskey at one dollar per bottle to the sailors and the Indians and it was recommended that the practice be stopped, as it caused trouble ashore.

Puget also noted — in reference to the Northern Indians — that "disease and distortion was apparently unknown to each of these tribes." He continues, "We never saw any scarred with wounds, a most convincing proof to my mind of their peacable disposition."

Clerke noted in his journal that the Indian men of Nootka had large knees, contracted calves and protruberant "ancles." He attributed these deformities to their sitting upon their legs in their canoes, concluding that "these people seldom leave the waterside but live a great deal in their canoes and supply themselves with the principal part of their provender from the water." Walkem relates that the Haidas of the Queen Charlotte Islands tended toward bowed legs and also attributed the cause to the long hours spent in canoes, beginning in early childhood.

15
Punishment

PENAL PRACTICES MAY SEEM, on the surface, somewhat beyond the scope of a medical discussion. It must be remembered, however, that the common method of punishment in the eighteenth century was by flogging. This procedure inflicted such lacerating injury to the victim's back that, were it to be administered to a "soft" citizen of the present century, hospitalization would undoubtedly be in order.[1] In those days, men were so inured to physical hardship that punishment by whipping, although painful, was considered a commonplace. At sea, only the barest details were recorded in the official log, usually at the end of the day's entry, a trifle among other trivia.

Nonetheless, flogging was a formal, almost ritualistic proceeding, to be carried out according to the King's Regulations on instruction of the captain, who determined a man's guilt and the number of strokes to be administered with little semblance of a trial. The ship's crew were mustered on deck to "witness punishment." The surgeon stood by, as well, in case he was needed to revive the man. The victim was then triced to a grating propped up at the gangway or Jacob's ladder leading to the quarter deck, and the whip was produced. Its nine thongs, each one inch thick and two feet long, were attached to a red handle. If the crime was thievery, a lash that had knots in it was used.

In the hands of an expert the cat-o'-nine-tails was a formidable weapon. Swung with finesse, the tips could be snapped with such speed that they broke through the sound barrier, emitting a spine-chilling crack. As a minimum, a dozen lashes were administered — with two, three, four or more dozen not uncommon, depending on the offence. They were laid across the appointed back by the husky boatswain's mate and he was relieved regularly, to ensure that fatigue did not interfere with his ardour. Typically, the very first lash cut deeply through the skin. After six lashes, the skin was completely raw. After two dozen, according to a contemporary writer, the back was so badly cut up and covered with blood in various stages of clotting that "it resembled roasted meat burnt nearly black before a scorching fire."

Little is recorded of any treatment received after such a punishment. It is presumed that some friends refreshed the bloodied back with that sailor's panacea — a few buckets of salt water. No doubt, for the more severe cases, salt packs were applied to reduce the swelling. The surgeon's main responsibility was to determine when the man was fit for duty.

The human back has thick skin. Relatively speaking, it is less sensitive than other parts of the body. Nonetheless, such treatment was grossly painful, and traumatic to the system as a whole. Characteristic transverse scars were left across the back of the rib cage, scars that are still seen occasionally to this day, for the lash remains a common form of punishment in some central European armies. The author came across such a devastated back soon after he graduated from medical school. The effect was so vivid that, more than two decades later, he instantly recognized a similarly scarred back when he saw it in Vancouver. There was no mistaking the mark of the cat-o'-nine-tails!

Vancouver ordered a number of punishments while working his way up the coast of the mainland. Most of the exploratory work was done in small boats that sailed up each inlet and estuary, as the search went on for the fabled passage from the Atlantic. Often the wind was down or wrong way to. Many miles had to be covered by back-breaking rowing of the heavy boats. The men must have become mightily tired and worn out, not only from the work itself but also from sleeping on the beaches or in the boats with little shelter from the weather. Most likely, the food, too, was worse than usual. The following excerpts from Puget's log of the *Discovery* would seem to indicate that the men were becoming more and more difficult to handle as they progressed northward. Their reaction seems understandable when one considers that Vancouver's men explored and charted more than ten thousand miles of coastline by oar.

13 July 1792 — Desolation Beach, De Fuca Straight, "Whales about ship. Punished John McArdle with 36 lashes for theft."

15 July 1792 — Mr. Johnstone's Passage out to Sea. " — Punished Richard Henly, seaman, with 48 lashes for disobeying an order."

27 July 1792 — Examination of De Fuca's Straight to Queen Charlottes Sound. " — Punished George Raybold, armorer, 48 lashes for neglect of duty, insolence, and contempt for his superior officers."

4 Aug. 1792 — From Deep Water Bluff to Queen Charlottes Sound. " — Punished Joseph Murgatroyd, carpenters mate, with 36 lashes and George Raybold, armorer, with 24 lashes for insolence."

5 Aug. 1792 — " — Mustered ships company and read the Articles of War."

7 Aug. 1792 — " — Ship went aground on Queen Charlotte Sound."

17 Aug. 1792 — At anchor, Safety Cove, Calvert Island. " — Punished James Englehart, sailmaker, with 48 lashes for embezzling the King's stores and Harry Hankins, pursers steward, with 12 lashes for the same offense."

18 Aug. 1792 — Same. " — Caught many salmon. Punished Isaac Wooden, seaman, with 36 lashes for theft."

Other lashings are recorded in the log of the *Discovery* but they are spaced out over a longer period of time. The number of punishments listed above for a period of little more than a month raises the suspicion that the men were being driven to the breaking point, a suspicion that tends to be confirmed by the reading of the Articles of War. When Vancouver turned back towards Nootka, with its promise of more civilized care and comfort, the frequency of punishments dropped back to normal.

Twentieth-century sensibilities may lead us to assume that a captain who resorted to the lash would be damned by his crew as a tyrant and brute. Such was not the case. Vancouver used the lash ninety-five times during his four and one-half year voyage and he was respected by all as a good captain and a fair disciplinarian.

One may wonder, however, that such strenuous punishment was not more of a deterrent to further transgression. Witness the case of George Raybold, recorded above, who received 48 lashes for insolence. Eight days later, with his back still raw, he received a further 24 lashes for the same offence. (Cook also recorded men who received more than one lashing.)

Clearly, to be a sailor was almost synonymous with hardship and pain. Yet the stoicism of these hard-bitten men had certain bounds. They were prepared to live under mind-numbing conditions, to be driven to the point of exhaustion, to accept as their companions sickness, injury, punishment and death by misadventure with little or no complaint. But when Richard Jones, seaman, fell from the main chains and was drowned during a gale that blew out some of the sails of the *Discovery*, they formally and severely criticized Captain Vancouver for not doing more than throw a grating overboard as a possible life raft. Captain Vancouver claimed that it was impossible to do more in such a gale and that the man had drowned immediately. The sailors' charge against Vancouver was eventually reviewed by the Admiralty and the claim was disallowed.

PART THREE

The 19th Century: Science Takes Hold

16

The Curtain Lifts

THE END OF THE EIGHTEENTH CENTURY marked a watershed in the history of modern, scientific medicine. In the entire period from the beginning of mankind to the year 1800, practical medicine had remained remarkably unchanged. Certainly, it had made a few gains in effectiveness. The honest physician still had little to offer that could compete with the far better established therapeutic principles of hope, hellfire and the power of faith. Nor could he, with his woefully inadequate weapons, do much to combat the glib tongue of the mercenary quack who preyed on those so desperately ill that they would follow anyone who promised them relief.

The hapless physician was constricted by his essential ignorance of the basic facts of human physiology, the etiology of disease and principles of treatment. In the centuries immediately preceding, however, the necessary scientific groundwork had begun to be laid. A great stride forward had been made in man's understanding of his own functioning when William Harvey described the circulation of the blood in the arteries and veins, discrediting the then current belief that the veins conducted the blood and the arteries the gaseous "humours of life." John Hunter, through his meticulously detailed dissection of cadavers, had so clarified the basic principles of surgical pathology as to establish surgery once and for all as a proper branch of scientific medicine. The death knell of scurvy had recently been sounded by James Lind and his controlled demonstrations of the prophylactic effects of lemon juice had, in turn, stimulated an interest in the science of nutrition. Jenner's cow-pox vaccine was proving that the deadly ravages of smallpox were preventable, and his success gave a powerful impetus to the study of the causes of infectious disease and the science of immunology.

Gradually, medical men began to place these and other discoveries at the service of their patients. But recognition of their efforts came slowly. The physician, although respected, had certainly not attained a position in his community comparable to that of his Pacific Northwest counterpart, the shaman.

As for the surgeon, he was still looked upon as a common artisan, for all his developing skills and growing responsibilities. It was natural that such an inferior status would cause some concern to the surgeons, and they took steps to remedy the situation. Their certifying body had been the poorly disciplined Company of Barber Surgeons, an organization formed in 1540 by the amalgamation of the blood-letting barbers and the bone-setting "cutting for stone" surgeons in an attempt to guard against the depredations of the quack. It served its purpose for a time, but it was a loosely knit alliance that toward the end did little to promote professional status or standards. Inevitably, in 1747, barber and surgeon went their separate ways. The surgeons formed the Company of Surgeons, to be supplanted in 1800 by the more responsible and ethical Royal College of Surgeons, counterpart of the established and respected Royal College of Physicians. The surgeons' College is the parent of the present Royal College of Surgeons of Canada.

As the new knowledge of physiology, pathology, bacteriology and the etiology of disease accumulated, so did the potential for preventing and curing a whole host of afflictions. But between the great pathfinder and the ordinary practitioner a gap lay open. In those days before telegraphy, rapid transit, audio-visual aids and computer-retrieval of information, the exchange of knowledge and experience was a laborious and haphazard process. A few informative medical journals were printed, but their data-gathering and distribution was limited by time, distance and cost.

How then to get word of new discoveries into the field? How to get work back of the practitioners' successes and failures with the new techniques? In answer, the physicians set up their own system of communications. Wherever aptitude allowed, the great discoverers became the great teachers. Those that listened assumed the function of disciples and, in their turn, spread the word wherever there were medical men to lend an ear. So effective was this word-of-mouth method of transmitting medical experience that teaching soon became an accepted obligation of the pioneering physician. It is an obligation that remains a basic ethic of the medical profession to this day.

The Stage is Set

THE GREAT ADVANCES IN MEDICAL DISCOVERY and teaching were largely European achievements, far removed from the sprawling and unorganized territory that was to become British Columbia. Yet it was this very remoteness that made the newly developing region a natural early proving ground for the newly developing medicine. No matter how eagerly the practising physician is on the lookout for the scientific discoveries that will increase his effectiveness as a healer, he tends in most circumstances to remain a conservative member of a conservative profession. New discoveries entail new risks, he has found; until experience has validated them, they may prove to have as great a potential for harm as for good. Such a natural conservatism often leads to a medical establishment which at times errs quite properly on the side of caution.

In the Pacific Northwest, such obstacles were few. The medical experience of the coast thus far had been limited to the mystical ministrations of the shaman, followed by a brief contact with the primitive medicine of the naval surgeon and the hygienist-captain. Nor did the few beneficial measures introduced by the latter two lead to an overabundance of confidence in their skill, for they tended to be submerged in the violent outbreaks of white man's vice and white man's disease among the susceptible natives.

Thus, with its prevailing medicine so inadequate and having no medical establishment to overcome, the embryonic province of British Columbia found itself ready and willing to take on as its own and vigorously apply the fledgling concepts of scientific medicine. The tendency was further reinforced by the character of the first land-based physicians to arrive in the area. It might have been expected that these men would be rejects from more civilized regions, in search of hardy settlements where their marginal abilities would be largely overlooked. Instead, the new arrivals turned out to be properly qualified physicians, with pioneer spirit to boot.

It was still not enough, in the Pacific Northwest of the early 1800's, to be "merely" a physician. It was a wild country, with great wealth waiting for those who were enterprising enough to tame it. Trade was the first order of the day, and it was as traders that the early physicians often earned their keep. The profit motive seemed hardly to figure in their efforts as healers. But if medicine was thus practised almost as a sideline, it was nevertheless practised conscientiously, with gifted hands and a trained and inquisitive intellect. New techniques were weighed, tested, applied, and the results noted. As English medicine progressed from an unskilled calling to a highly technical life-saving profession, British Columbia's physicians and surgeons kept pace with that progress, at times even surpassing the mother country by making vital discoveries of their own.

Inevitably, as the century wore on, medicine became too complex to remain a part-time preoccupation. And, as the physician's status as physician rose, so did the pitch of the con men, the quacks, and the quasi-medical graduates from diploma-mill schools. To guard against their abuses, and to set standards of medical practice, a certifying body was required, and this function was assumed by the British Columbia College of Physicians and Surgeons.

In summary, the nineteenth century became a "Cinderella" century for medicine in British Columbia. It started off with medical practice in low repute, a haphazard and ill-informed calling subordinated to the demands of botany or trade. It ended with a high standard of medical care. And, as the health and vigour of the citizen improved, so did the health and vigour of the medical profession.

Two Gentlemen in the Fur Trade

As has been seen, there was little land-based activity by the white man on the British Columbia coast during the first three decades of the century. The Russians were trading to the north in the area that is now known as Alaska. The Spaniards were settling to the south in Mexico and lower California. American trailblazers were beginning to make their way across the continent from the east. It would be a few years yet before the lure of California gold initiated their great covered-wagon migrations.

Between the Russians to the north and the Spanish to the south lay a wild and rugged land, good only for the trapping of furs. Into this region the Hudson's Bay Company gradually sent its traders. It had made its way to the mouth of the Columbia River and set up an establishment at Fort Vancouver. With the expansion of the population to the south, the Hudson's Bay Company turned northward. Its first post in the British Columbia area went up in 1827, at Fort Langley. This was followed by the building of Fort Victoria on Vancouver Island. Several other forts were strategically placed on the coast, to facilitate the trading of furs with the Indians. The building of these forts marked the true beginning of the white man's settlement on the coast.

It was the enlightened policy of the Hudson's Bay Company to station a man with medical training at one of the forts. The first man sent turned out to be a native Canadian. John Frederick

Kennedy, a metis, was the oldest son of Alexander Kennedy, a Scot who was master of the Hudson's Bay Company post of Cumberland House in what is now the province of Saskatchewan.[1] After he grew up, the young Kennedy took medical training and became a Licentiate of the Royal College of Surgeons of Edinburgh in September, 1829. He was then engaged by the Hudson's Bay Company as a surgeon in the Columbia district of the northwest coast of America at a salary of £60 per annum. He served for a time under Dr. McLoughlin at Fort Vancouver and in 1831 was posted north to Naas (Fort Simpson), near the operations of the Russian American Trading Company. Little has been recorded about his work at Fort Simpson, and later at Fort Rupert, other than a report that describes him as "being careful and attentive, and qualified to act as trader, storekeeper or accountant in addition to his medical duties." Eventually, he was appointed Chief Trader.

In 1856, after his retirement, Kennedy was elected as a representative from Nanaimo to the first House of Assembly to sit in Victoria for the Colony of Vancouver Island. It is interesting to note that of the seven members of the Assembly, two were medical men — the other being John Sebastian Helmcken. Kennedy did not serve for long. The *Victoria Gazette* for April 5, 1859 reports: "Hon. Dr. John Frederick Kennedy, Member of the House of Assembly for Nanaimo, departed this life on Sunday last. — " The obituary cites his good work as a surgeon over a period of twenty years and goes on to remark on his great value as a negotiator of treaties with the Indians, attributing his success to his having their confidence.

In 1834, three years after Kennedy was posted to Fort Simpson, another man with medical training was sent north by the Hudson's Bay Company from Fort Vancouver. He was William Fraser Tolmie, a surgeon, and because of his ability he, too, was eventually appointed Chief Trader.[2] Fortunately for posterity, this intelligent and methodical Scotsman kept a diary from which may be obtained some insight into the way of life of one of the earliest medical men on the coast. Tolmie's notes on the medical cases he encountered and the treatment that was administered —

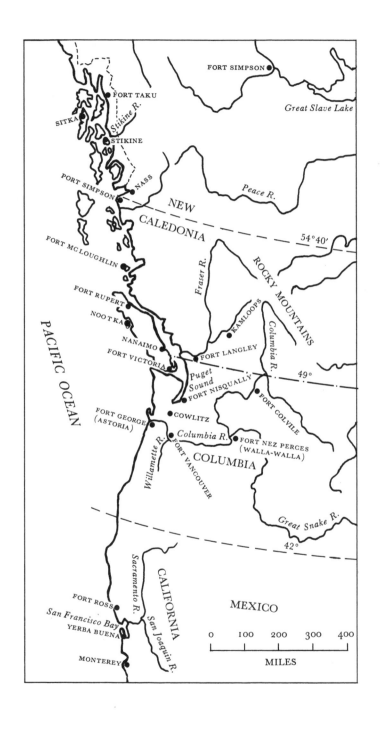

FORT SIMPSON

Great Slave Lake

FORT TAKU

SITKA

Stikine R.

STIKINE

PORT SIMPSON • NASS

NEW
CALEDONIA

Peace R.

54°40'

FORT McLOUGHLIN

Fraser R.

ROCKY MOUNTAINS

FORT RUPERT

NOOTKA

KAMLOOPS

NANAIMO

FORT VICTORIA

FORT LANGLEY

Columbia R.

49°

*Puget
Sound*

FORT NISQUALLY

FORT COLVILE

PACIFIC OCEAN

FORT GEORGE
(ASTORIA)

• COWLITZ

Columbia R.

FORT NEZ PERCES
(WALLA-WALLA)

COLUMBIA

Willamette R.

FORT VANCOUVER

Great Snake R.

42°

Sacramento R.

CALIFORNIA

MEXICO

FORT ROSS

San Francisco Bay
YERBA BUENA

San Joaquin R.

MONTEREY

0   100   200   300   400

MILES

as well as his descriptions of incidents in the daily life of a Chief Fur Trader — make of his diary a valuable historical document. Twenty three years old when he arrived, he was a rugged man in charge of a rugged outpost, surrounded by a strange and, at times, hostile people. Yet his frequent notes and remarks on the classical and medical literature indicate that he was one of the new breed of surgeons, no longer content with being an artisan but a scholar in search of the knowledge that would inform the work of his hands.

Tolmie had atttended the University of Glasgow. After his second year he left the University, and there is no record of his graduation or of his becoming a Licentiate of the Faculty of Physicians and Surgeons of Glasgow. Soon afterward, he signed on with the Hudson's Bay Company as surgeon, and set sail for Fort Vancouver on the Columbia River. He describes the voyage via the Sandwich Islands as a "pilgrimage" of nearly eight months. Several more months were spent under the tutelage of an outstanding medical man, John McLoughlin, who doubled as Chief Factor of Fort Vancouver. Then Tolmie was sent north to Fort McLoughlin, situated at what is now Bella Bella on Millbank Sound.

The wall around the fort was ruggedly built with heavy logs, overshadowing the several small houses inside. Amenities were few. The staple articles of diet were dried salmon and venison, with other game on occasion. Supplies, along with mail and trade goods, were brought by the Hudson's Bay trading vessels that arrived periodically to carry off the harvest of the furs. The weather was wet and cold and the natives of the area were disturbed at times to the point of violence by these white settlers from another world. In the circumstance, it was necessary that a medical man have qualities somewhat different from the gentle touch and kindly disposition that are expected of his present-day brother. That Tolmie had the necessary attributes may be gleaned from the following extract from his diary:

Thursday, February 13th, 1834: Charbonneau, a rascally Canadian noted for laziness & dishonesty (having repeatedly been detected in acts of fraud) was this morning informed on, as having converted the space behind my house into a Temple of Cloacina, when disturbed after dusk & of publicly boasting of his audacious filthiness. I thought it right to make an example of him to the others & accordingly after breakfast on encountering him saluted his seat of honour, the offending member with a hearty kick & his mug with a whack which drew claret. I repeated the applications once or twice & at length he grappled & scratched my face in several places. Just as I was going to try a trip, Mr. Manson came up and hurled the fellow to the earth and another kick in the posterior completed his punishment — .

Another entry would seem to indicate that Tolmie was prepared to defend his honour against assault from nobler quarters as well, as expected of a young gentleman of those days:

Wednesday, March 5th, 1834: All day moving about the Fort or sitting in the door of Bastion. Reading the article Dueling is the Young Man's Best Companion — (by the way) made one trip to Point Portlock — tonight Guthrie on Spain.

The problem that could be created by an aching tooth before the advent of painless dentistry is illustrated by Tolmie's notes, when he himself was so afflicted. In Glasgow, Tolmie had been taught how to remove teeth and was prepared to undertake this procedure, should a case present itself. Unfortunately, however, "physician heal thyself" is a maxim that does not properly take into account the particular perspective and leverage that must be brought to bear on the extraction of a troublesome molar. After several days of severe toothache, Tolmie notes:

Tuesday, April 29th: Large flocks of geese and cranes still passing. Trouble with toothache and got temporary relief by smoking and this evening more permanent ease by the application of a heated probe to the exposed nervous surface — since then the tooth has been free from pain, but have felt more twinges along the cheek.

Wednesday, April 30th: Toothache less troublesome.

Thursday, May 1st, 1834: Toothache very painful — had the actual cautery applied by means of a piece of iron wire — it diminished the pain in the tooth, but has irritated the different branches of the 7th pair, and I have since suffered pain in the cheek, ear and temple of the same side. Occupied all day in making a set of Apothecaries' Weights. The anniversary of my arrival at the Columbia.

Friday, May 2nd — finished the set of weights. Toothache continues — pressure on the affected tooth causes excruciating pain extending backwards to ear. Reading Shakespear.

Saturday, May 3rd: Looking after axemen at work at Point Duncan and reading King Lear, which is deeply interesting. Toothache is better.

The entry of the following day is worth quoting from a medical point of view. It suggests two conclusions: One is that venereal disease was flourishing among the Indians; the second, that Tolmie had some sort of series of medical, therapeutic textbooks with him to which he could refer when faced with a problem unfamiliar to him.

Sunday, May 4th: Reading Abernethy on Strictures, having an Indian affected with Stricture and disease of Testes as a patient. Tonight Dwight. (Author's Note: Dwight is mentioned several times as the author of a volume containing religious items such as "personal preaching of Christ" and the story of Ruth.)

Not long after Tolmie arrived at Fort McLoughlin, he was visited by some Indians with wounds on their forearms. The lesions intrigued Tolmie, from a medical point of view and otherwise, as their etiology was a human bite.

The story concerned Wacash, a powerful chief of a nearby tribe of Indians. Most likely, he was a shaman, for he was said to be able to conjure and do other things that shamans did. He lived by himself and was reputed to dine on human flesh. On occasion and as a special favour, he could be induced to bite some of the flesh from an Indian's arm. It was the wounds from these bites that Tolmie was to examine and they had been carefully covered with softened cedar bark and tied in place with thongs of the same material. On removal of the bandage, it was apparent that several square inches of skin and subcutaneous tissue had been bitten out.

In a sequel to this story, Tolmie relates that, at a later date, Wacash began to vomit blood. After doing so for several days, he

99

turned to his white confrere for help. It was at this point that the realist in Tolmie came to the fore. He refused to treat the Indian, aware that, if his patient died, the latter's relatives might come seeking Tolmie's life in retribution.

Tolmie further demonstrates his prudence in such matters. He notes that, when required to provide medicine to an Indian of some importance about whose illness he knew little, he gave him peppermint, an innocuous placebo that might mobilize the patient's faith while doing him little harm.

In 1834, as Tolmie was travelling on board ship to Fort Simpson, he undertook what must have been one of the earliest modern operations performed on the coast. There was a seaman aboard from the recently wrecked ship *Vancouver* and Tolmie notes in his diary:

Sunday, June 15th: Naas Straits near Pellys' Cove. . . . Busy during week writing home and arranging medicines — on Monday removed a fatty tumor from the breast of one of the *Vancouver*'s crew — it was the size of a large orange, but was unfortunately lost. Incision transverse — vessels secured by torsion — the man is doing well.[3]

Tolmie also carried on a practice by correspondence, a somewhat doubtful enterprise, as the mail often took six months to be delivered. All the same, in a letter dated June 24, 1837, to one Sam Black, living in the Okanagan, Tolmie gives some advice that would do credit to a modern-day practitioner:

I send a phial of which, when the pain is troublesome 30 drops may be taken in water as often as three or four times in the course of the twenty-four hours — also some tonic pills of which one should be swallowed every morning on getting up — and some lax pills similar to those of last year. Besides using these medicines, I would recommend your adopting the following regime — get up about two hours before breakfast and if the weather and season be favourable, walk two or three miles at a gentle pace. Take one or two short walks in the course of the day and retire to bed at an early hour. Use such articles of diet as you find to agree best with your stomach. Make four light meals daily and endeavour to rise from each meal with some slight remaining appetite.

Such are the disciplined writings of one of the earliest representatives of the medical profession to live and practise on the west coast of Canada. His diary includes not only the workaday happenings of his position as a fur trader, it details the studious observations of a devoted botanist and naturalist. The medical notes are few and far between, primarily because his panel of practice was limited ordinarily to the few white and native employees of the Hudson's Bay Company.

Tolmie's diary also serves to paint a portrait of the character, personality and ability of its author. He appears to be a determined Scotsman, young by modern day standards, but quite capable of handling his affairs and taking care of himself. His qualities of self-reliance are demonstrated in his solution to the problem of his unruly subordinate during his first days at Fort McLoughlin. Another incident that demonstrated his courage occurred at Fort Simpson. He reports that some Indians became intoxicated. One apparently seized a barrel of goods and was defending it with a dagger. Tolmie took a cutlass and bore down on him, so intimidating the thief and his friends that the loot was given up without a struggle.

Though he was a bachelor and speaks at times of his loneliness, he declined to emulate his fellows and enter upon a "marriage" of convenience. Apparently, he had whatever it took to resist the blandishments of the Indian maidens. In his diary, he philosophizes about his isolation:

Wednesday, December 10 (1834): Yesterday and today Indians have kept me in employment until dusk. In the evening read a volume of Trait's Travel. Have of late & perhaps always been too negligent in journalizing the subjects of my thoughts and meditations. Since coming here what most frequently had been a matter of cogitation, is the dullness of this place & of life in the "Pays Sauvage" in general. Entirely deprived of society even of equals, not to speak of the benefits arising from intercourse with one's superiors in knowledge and wisdom — the ideas are seldom raised to objects of a lofty nature but tend to assimilate themselves with those of the person's most frequently met with viz. — the wretched Aborigines. The pleasure of polished female society we are obliged to forego & all this for filthy lucre's sake.

Three Journals of Practice

THROUGH THE MIDDLE OF THE NINETEENTH CENTURY, a mere handful of land-based medical men found their way to the Pacific Northwest. These continued to share the burden of health care along the coast with their naval brethren, the sea surgeons. A good index to the changing medical practices of the times may be had by a glance at the few Royal Naval Surgeons Journals of Practice that have come down to us.

The surgeons' journals of Captains Cook and Vancouver have been lost, as have so many of the older journals. One of the earliest to survive is the 1791 journal of the *Chatham*. Another, written near the time that Kennedy and Tolmie were practising, is the journal of the *Blossom*. Finally, there is the 1852 journal of the *Thetis*.

The Surgeon's Journal of *His Majesty's Hospital Ship Chatham* is written in 1791 by Mr. Hugh Weeks, Surgeon. He is an artisan type of surgeon and does not yet qualify as an officer and a gentleman. His journal is a simple affair, each case being recorded in one line across the page. In that line is stated the patient's name, his rank on his ship and his age. (The journals of the active ships often noted as well whether or not he had been pressed into service.) The diagnosis is very brief, being simply "broken leg," or "itch," or "cough" and mention of treatment is similarly brief. There is a final set of columns where a tick indicates whether or not the man died, returned to duty, or was otherwise disposed of.

The Journal of Practice of *HMS Blossom* was written in 1823 by Mr. Peter McDougall, acting surgeon.[1] His qualifications for the position of ship's surgeon must have been rather more substantial, for he was considered an officer and a gentleman and, therefore, was granted quarter-deck rank. He had been certified by the Royal College of Surgeons. His records show the earliest indications of history-taking and descriptive notes. The routine name and rank appear together with other miscellaneous data. The medical part is still short, but it is more descriptive. For instance, he describes one patient as of "full habit and florid complexion. Has since yesterday been affected with pain in the left side of the thorax and under the left scapula, in breathing respiration are much aggravated on making any sudden exertion of voice or body. Pulse natural, general health does not suffer — belly regular." His treatments are more elaborate than before and are well recorded. He wrote his prescriptions and the directions in Latin and some of his medicines are still in use today.

In 1852, *Her Majesty's Frigate Thetis* visited Esquimalt and the Queen Charlotte Islands. On the face of the Journal of Practice is the name of the surgeon. The routine printed "Mr." has been scratched out and the name John Douglas, M.D. as surgeon is written. Though less than thirty years have elapsed since McDougall's record, the differences are notable.[2]

For the first time, proper histories and physical findings are recorded as a matter of course and daily progress notes are made. While in British Columbia waters, his records show some cases of pneumonia, treated by bleeding for the fever, opiates for the distress and counter-irritants for relief of the pleuritic pain. He notes the bleeding in Latin as "flat venesectio ad oz. XVI." Following the removal of the blood, he liked to report a "satisfactory syncope," as this was apparently considered a good sign. The blood itself was left in the glass cupping bowl and it was noted whether it "cupped and buffed," a reference to the formation of a normal cup-shaped clot with a buff-coloured coat. The clot was called the crassamentum and sepsis, scurvy and other diseases were known to create specific and recognizable changes in it that were used as diagnostic aids. He also reported a case of gout, which he successfully treated with aperients and a colchicum mixture. On the return voyage from the Queen Charlotte Islands to Esquimalt, seaman Patrick Menehin, age 24, "fell dead whilst in the act of handing up a tub from the hold." The details of the death and the post-mortem findings are recorded clearly. The man had died of a massive hemorrhage following the perforation of an inflamed ulcerated aorta.[3]

But the future of medicine lay ashore. There, the territory continued to be dominated by the Hudson's Bay Company. In 1850, it hired and brought from England a man who belonged to an entirely new species of physician. He was a Diplomate of the Royal College of Surgeons, a member of the Royal College of Physicians and a Licentiate of the Apothecaries' Society of England. During his training at Guy's Hospital, he had witnessed the whole range of surgical procedures, minor and major, all performed without an anaesthetic. Subsequently, he had been on hand to observe one of the first operations to be performed under the new general anaesthetic, ether. He was by far the best trained and the best qualified physician and surgeon ever to appear at Fort Victoria.

His name was John Sebastian Helmcken. With him, a new standard of medical care was introduced to the coast. Insofar as the healer's art was concerned, it was the beginning of modern times. It is a measure of the youth of modern health care in British Columbia that the province still contains people who started life as patients of Doctor Helmcken.

Copy
of
Daily Sick List
of
Her Majesty's Ship Thetis

From 1st July 1851
To 30th September 1852.

John Douglas M.D. Surgeon.

Entry	Name	Age	Quality	Disease	Discharge	How Disposed of	No. of Days Sick
1851 July 1	Willm Shute	19	Ord:	Bruised Toe	July 13	Duty	12
" "	John Winter	19	Boy 2d Class	Abscess	" 13	Duty	12
" "	Mr Henry Lloyd	15	Cadet	Cynanche Tons	" 20	Duty	19
" "	Mr John Sangster	25	Lieut: R.M.	Ulcer	Augt 18	Duty	48
" "	Fred: Davis	27	Marine	Fracture	July 7	Duty	6
" "	Chas Leathlean	23	Sailmr Crew	Bubo Syphilit	Sept 21	Duty	82
" "	Mr Geo Strong	20	Midshipm	Sprained ankle	July 2	Duty	1
" "	Chas Mitchell	24	Ord	Cut Forehead	" 13	Duty	12
" "	Benjn Baker	33	Dr.master	Rheumatism	Augt 3	Duty	33
" 2	Willm Thomas	38	Boatsw. Mate	Pleuritis	July 13	Duty	11
" "	Willm L Mays	25	Seaman School-master	Syphilis	Sept 24	Invalided	84
" 5	Mr Arthur Sansum	37	Lieut:	Gout	July 9	Duty	4
" 8	Mr Willm Power	15	Cadet	Ulcer	" 15	Duty	7
" 11	Edwin Bevens	20	Ord:	Contusion	" 20	Duty	9
" "	James Miller	27	A.B.	Bubo Symp:	Nov: 15	Duty	127
" 15	Edmd Nash	20	Ord:	Ulcer	July 18	Duty	3
" 17	Robt Cundy	20	Boy 1st Class	Phlegmone	" 24	Duty	7
" 24	Thos Clark	26	A.B.	Rheumatism	Augt 18	Duty	25
" 28	Walter Pope	39	A.B.	Catarrh	July 31	Duty	3
" 30	Henry Darke	50	A.B.	Contusion	Augt 10	Duty	11

arrival it appeared on board and only 23 cases were added to the list though several more were affected in a slighter degree. The general symptoms were, a feeling of lassitude & debility, headache, sneezing, pain in eyes, back & limbs; sore throat & hoarseness, white tongue, a hard dry cough & a sense of rawness & pain in chest, griping in epigastrium: About the 3rd or 4th day the headache & cough became easier, the sense of rawness being followed by expectoration, the skin becoming relaxed and all the symptoms mitigated. The treatment consisted of an aperient of Pil: Hydrarg: & Ext: Colocynth Comp: followed by saline diaphoretics with Antimon: Potass. Tart: every four hours, and in cases where the cough continued urgent, Tinct. Camphor: Comp: Vin: Antimon: & Tinct: Scillæ was given: a few cases required the application of a blister to the chest.

Cynanche Tonsil:— The case remaining from last Journal proved obstinate and a part of the left tonsil was excised. He has suffered no inconvenience since.

Palpitation of Heart— occurred in a young delicate Marine who had suffered from the affection previously: he had irregular action of heart with intermitting pulse, no symptoms of organic disease could be detected. Tonics of Sulph: Ferri & Quinia were prescribed with beneficial effect & he was discharged to Duty, but six months afterwards he returned labouring under the same symptoms having been longer than usual on salt provisions: He was again put under Tonics and a better diet allowed and the symptoms gradually yielded.

Hæmorrhois— Cases presenting nothing important.

Rupture of Aorta— This is the case of a seaman Patrick Menehen æt 24 who suddenly dropped down while in the act of handing up a tub from the hold, he was seen immediately and found dead. On examining the chest next day, the pericardium was much distended, on opening it a little serum escaped and a large clot of dark coagulated blood surrounded the heart; this being carefully removed an opening admitting the little finger was found in the posterior part of the aorta a little above its origin: on slitting up the aorta there appeared on the internal coat a patch about two inches long & one broad having a puckered pitted surface, on the lower part of this was the opening through all the coats with smooth edges, and on the upper part of this patch was another opening about the size of a pea through the internal coat, it had ragged undermined edges & extended into the middle coat which was soft and of a reddish hue. There was no deposition of cartilage or bony scales on the serous coat, nor were any clots of blood or fibrine deposited near the large opening, and no dilatation of the external coat. The ulceration had formed through all the coats when the fatal event occurred on the 15th August.

Syphilis & Bubo — These were treated in the usual way, some of the buboes proved tedious & obstinate: a case of secondary symptoms in the form of blotches in a marine who stated that he had been several times under treatment for chancres. He was put under the Bichlorid: Hydrarg: & Infus: Cinchon:, the spots being touched with diluted citrine ointment; and the disease disappeared. And ther case of secondary symptoms in John Mays æt. 25 seaman schoolmaster was invalided at Valparaiso on 24th Sept: /51. About the middle of May he complained of pain in the shin of right leg which was red, swelled & tender, he then stated that about six years ago when in China he had several venereal sores which he attempted to cure himself & that they existed a considerable time, he did not then take any mercury: before joining this ship in July 1850 he contracted a fresh disease for which he took mercury & his mouth became slightly sore. The treatment on board consisted of the application of blisters to the shin & the administration of mercury, under the influence of which he was kept for a fortnight and the pain & swelling disappeared. He again returned about the beginning of July with the same symptoms much aggravated, the pain being very severe during the night; the Bichloride of Mercury was again prescribed in small doses three times a day, blisters applied to the shin & anodynes given at night to procure sleep; this failing calomel & opium was given twice a day & he was kept under its influence for a month without benefit or relief; the mercury was then omitted and a mixture of Iodid: Potassii Liq: Potass: & Infus: Cinchon: prescribed & continued for a month, a blister being applied occasionally to the shin & anodynes given at bedtime; this afforded little or no relief, the pain still continuing with considerable thickening of the periosteum, & the same symptoms beginning to appear in the other leg, all treatment having failed in checking or even relieving the disease I considered him a fit case for Hospital treatment in England.

Orchitis — These cases following gonorrhœa yielded to the usual treatment, one case of chronic enlargement with hydrocele in right testicle was tapped in August last and relieved, no injection was used on account of the chronic disease; he afterwards returned with the testicle more enlarged but it contained no fluid, a palliative treat=

John Helmcken, Family Physician

IN 1850, THE GESTATION PERIOD for the infant British Columbia was drawing to an end. In 1849, Vancouver Island had become a Crown colony. The following year, the population of the whole island totalled 450 whites of all nationalities, with most of them in and around the capital, Fort Victoria, and the adjacent area, Sooke. During the next decade, word of gold discoveries on the mainland filtered south to California. With the onset of gold fever, the population swelled. Concern at the influx of "strangers" hastened the amalgamation of the Crown colony of Vancouver Island and the mainland, and the united colony of British Columbia was born in 1866. Five years later, in return for a promise to take over its public works debt and to make Burrard Inlet the western terminus of a transcontinental railway, it became a province of the new Dominion of Canada.

These formative years of the lusty new province were formative for the medical profession, as well. Few tangible new techniques had made their appearance between 1800 and 1850, other than such supplementary aids to physical examination as the stethoscope and the art of percussing resonant areas to determine the presence of pathology. But after 1850, medicine and surgery moved forward with increasing speed.

It was a golden age for doctor-patient relationships, for the pioneer ethic encouraged the closest adherence to the Hippocratic

Oath. Typically, the pioneer physician ministered to his far-flung flock with little regard for his comfort or monetary reward. Doctor Helmcken speaks of treating the miners in their tent town, simply because they were in need. Doctor W. W. Walkem recounts a journey that took several days by canoe to the end of the north arm of Burrard Inlet to treat a man with an injured leg. Doctor A. W. S. Black was killed by a fall from his horse, as he rode from New Westminster to Vancouver in the dark hours of the early morning to answer a call for his services.[1] It is recorded time and again that no charges were made where a patient was in poor financial circumstances.

For a long time, the physician continued to depend primarily on his five senses, but he was learning to use them astutely, and to translate them into a sixth sense — judgment. He questioned his patient in great detail as to the onset of his illness. With the known facts of the case, he developed its history. He observed the general condition of the patient, looking for the wasting of muscles, the signs of loss of weight, the flush of a fever, the signs of laboured breathing, or the facies of those tormented by pain. He smelled the breath searching for pathological odours, such as the fecal smell of large bowel obstruction, the characteristic odour of uremia, or the sharp smell of acidosis. In the absence of X-rays, he percussed the cavities of the body to obtain any information a change in resonance would give. With his crudely made stethoscope, he listened to the sounds of the active organs within the body. He felt the forehead for heat and the skin of the body for dryness. He wiped up the sweat on a finger and smelled it, and even tasted it, to determine the presence or absence of abnormal toxic excretions from the blood. He looked at the oral cavity and felt the tongue as a measure of dehydration of the patient's body. He held a glass of urine to the light to look for the cloudiness of blood or pus and he tasted it as a test for possible diabetes. When need be, he scraped his fingers along a bar of soap to fill his nail beds and then examined the fundamental orifices of the body to gain every bit of information that was obtainable. At the conclusion of his examination, he sat beside his patient and, thoughtfully continuing his observation, he attempted to add up his findings in the light of his training, his experience and reports of recent discoveries so as to arrive at a reasonable diagnosis and to determine the necessary treatment.

This was the tradition to which Doctor Helmcken belonged and, as the population of the colony grew, so did his practice. He soon found that he had to learn how to ride a horse and manage a canoe, so that he could pay "house calls" on some of his local patients. He also accepted the care of those in more remote areas. Soon after his arrival, Doctor Helmcken could claim to be "the leading practitioner from San Francisco to the North Pole and from Asia to the Red River of the North." Fortunately, his "territory" was sparsely settled. Nonetheless, he did take on responsibility for the men living in the hinterland, such as those stationed at the various Hudson's Bay trading posts. These men possessed little or no medical knowledge or skill. The medicines that were sent had to be divided into their proper doses and labelled with explicit directions. Accordingly, as the good doctor relates, he had to make up so many dozen purges, so many dozen pukes (medicine was a vigorous science in those days), so many doses of quinine or calomel, and send off these deadly missiles to wreak their havoc. Apparently, no casualties were reported, though whether this was due to the doctor's skill or the rugged constitutions of the pioneers is not stated.

At least one contemporary treatment required no chemotherapy whatever, as the *British Colonist* of February 20, 1871, reports it:

Influenza — Nearly every person one meets wheeze's like a blacksmith's bellows with a hole in the leather. A 'suffering brother,' who has tried it, recommends the cold water cure. He says that he swathed his chest and head in wet towels, went to bed and covered himself with blankets. Soon a profuse perspiration set in, the choked, stifled sensation left his nose and throat and he fell into a quiet sleep. In the morning when he awoke the influenze had disappeared.

It was not long before other doctors arrived to share Dr. Helmcken's burdens. One of these, John Chapman Davie, had a son who was medically inclined. After graduating in 1865 from Cooper Medical College in San Francisco, he joined his father in practice in Victoria. Doctor J. C. Davie, Jr. took up surgery and soon Doctor Helmcken and the younger Davie became a well known team of physician and surgeon. Doctor Davie, Jr. was an energetic man and a keen surgeon. He introduced the Lister antiseptic spray to the Royal Jubilee and the St. Joseph's Hospitals in Victoria, and later became one of the foremost proponents of aseptic surgical techniques. He studied his cases carefully and kept statistics which enabled him, at a meeting of the British Columbia Medical Association in Vancouver in 1898 or 1899, to report on a series of one hundred appendectomies that he had performed. The audience was small, but in it was Sir Michael Foster, Professor of Physiology at Cambridge University, who was then en route to San Francisco to deliver the Lane series of lectures. Apparently, it was the accepted custom in England not to operate early in "perityphilitis" (as appendicitis was often called in those days). Doctor Davie prefaced his paper with some characteristically forthright remarks. "I am English myself," he said, "and give way to no man in my admiration of British practice, but when it comes to the treatment of appendicitis, they don't know a damn thing about it." It is reported that Sir Michael stroked his beard and said nothing, but looked a little surprised. Doctor Davie proceeded to read his paper, pointing out that adherence to the principle of early operation in all cases of appendicitis would result in a lowering of mortality. Experience has proved him right.

The work of blasting a right-of-way through the mountains for the coming transcontinental Canadian Pacific Railway was a rugged undertaking of heroic proportions. Typically, typhoid and Rocky Mountain fever took their toll, their fatalities ranking alongside those attributed to black powder and dynamite. Doctor H. E. Langis writes of his experiences as a medical officer on the railway at Yale.[2]

In April, 1885, I took (Dr.) Hanington's place and had for field of duty, from Port Moody to Savona. We had a small hospital (12 beds) at Yale and with very little apparatus had to furnish our own surgical instruments. The accommodation was very scant and when we had to perform under anaesthesia, the only anaesthetist available was the steward and head nurse and, in my time, only nurse who would administer chloroform under the vigilant eye of the performer.

Anyhow, we had very few mishaps and bad results, as the contractors, in blasting, would kill their men outright and do very little injury to those who fell under our care. In the fall of 1885 we all came to Granville, which a few months afterwards, was going to be Vancouver — .

Though Langis' report may indicate a certain lack of concern for the life of the workers, we have the word of Mr. J. E. Griffith, Deputy Minister and Chief Engineer of Railways in the Department of Railways, Victoria, that "I have no reason to think that the number of deaths on the Canadian Pacific Railway construction was anything near as large as reported on the other continental railways to the south —."

Although the doctor was a busy man, primarily concerned with his practice, he often found himself embroiled in public affairs. This was the natural consequence, perhaps, of his university education and his familiarity with the problems of the people in the colony. Few of the miners, loggers, farmers, and fur traders had seen the inside of a university, and few had visited both the tents and shacks of the poor and the fine homes of the wealthy. Soon after Doctor Helmcken's arrival he became interested in the local politics and, when the 1856 elections were held for the first House of Assembly on Vancouver Island, he was elected as a member for Esquimalt. Subsequently, he was chosen from among the seven duly elected members to be the first Speaker of the House. He alone was re-elected to the second House and, again, to the third House, in 1863. He continued in this position until 1866, when the Colony of Vancouver Island was formally united with the newer Colony of Columbia on the mainland.

As the population of the colony grew, more and more medical practitioners arrived. Pressure mounted to have the medical profession organized, and in 1867 what was termed "an ordinance respecting practitioners in medicine and surgery" was passed in the then-capital of New Westminster. As its objective, it states that "it is expedient that persons requiring medical aid should be enabled to distinguish between qualified and unqualified practitioners. . . ."

The ordinance provided for the appointment of a registrar, outlined his duties and designated who might be registered. The requirements were relatively high for the time:[3]

Any person, being possessed of any diploma, licence or privilege to practise medicine or surgery from any school, college, society or faculty of medicine or surgery, either in the United Kingdom or in a foreign country, such a school, college, society or faculty requiring a compulsory course of study, extending over not less than three years, such a person shall on payment of a fee of Ten Dollars be entitled to be registered, etc., provided always, that nothing in this ordinance shall be so construed as to prevent anyone, possessing a diploma, who is now practising in this colony from continuing to practise as heretofore, — .

Seeing in the ordinance a challenge to her authority, Great Britain objected, claiming the right for her physicians and surgeons to practise in any of the colonies. After debate, the final authority was kept by the Registrar in the new colony. The first registry contained thirty-nine names.

The ordinance continued in force until the medical act of 1886 established the College of Physicians and Surgeons, governed by a council representing the medical profession of the province.

In a further attempt to upgrade health standards in the new province, an "ordinance for promoting public health in the colony of British Columbia" was passed in 1869. It was aimed primarily at controlling the not infrequent epidemics of infectious diseases and provided for the appointment of an extraordinary officer to be called the Health Officer, to act during a health crisis, such as a serious epidemic. Such a crisis apparently arose in July, 1892, and the health officer in Vancouver, backed by the mayor and other city officials, proved most zealous in his efforts to keep Vancouver from being infected.

The story begins with the arrival of the Canadian Pacific steamship *Empress of China* at Albert Head, the quarantine station outside Victoria, with smallpox aboard. The routine precautions and isolation of the sick were carried out, and the liner proceeded to Vancouver to discharge her remaining passengers and cargo.

Enter a Vancouver lass named Ella, reputed to be a member of the "oldest profession." Practising that profession in Vancouver, she apparently had contact with an incubating case of smallpox off the ship and became herself, in turn, a carrier. She then travelled to Victoria and, while "moonlighting" there, apparently infected a young man. Upon her return to Vancouver, the pustular rash appeared on her. As might have been expected, Vancouver officials claimed she got the smallpox from her Victoria paramour, whereas Victoria asserted that she had given the disease to that young man. In the meantime, an epidemic had started to spread in Victoria. None appeared in Vancouver.

Health officials in the mainland city immediately quarantined all Victoria citizens and, on the arrival from Victoria of the steamship *Yosemite*, would permit no one ashore, whether vaccinated or not. Fire hoses were played on the gangway to keep the passengers aboard ship and any cargo landed was thoroughly fumigated with burning sulphur. Victoria became hostile. An injunction was issued against the Vancouver city officials, signed by Mr. Justice Crease of Victoria. The paper, however, was not accepted until it had been thoroughly and ostentatiously fumigated with sulphur. Pursuant to the injunction, Vancouver's Mayor Cope, City Solicitor St. George Hammersley and City Health Officer Joe Huntley were arrested and lodged in the Vancouver Hotel, while awaiting transport to Victoria to stand trial. In Victoria, the final decision of the court was to release them with a warning. They were, it concluded, only doing what they considered to be their duty. . . .

British Columbia had one false start before establishing its first functioning hospital. The cause, of all things, was the Crimean War between England, France and Turkey on one side and Russia on the other. Although the Northeast Pacific Ocean area had been declared a neutral zone, Governor Douglas built a complete naval hospital at Esquimalt in 1855. It was to receive any casualties that might result from a planned British and French naval attack on the Russian Colony of Petropauloviki on the eastern side of the Kamchatka Peninsula. As the Russians had withdrawn before the allied fleet arrived, no casualties materialized. The only patient ever to be treated in the hospital was an engineer of the returning fleet who was suffering from scurvy.

The first functioning hospital to be established on the coast came into being under circumstances that a present-day hospital board member would consider unusual. The undertaking must be attributed to a layman, Reverend E. Cridge of Victoria, Chaplain of the Hudson's Bay Company. In a brief monograph entitled "Pioneer Days," Cridge recalls the occasion:[4]

It was in 1858 that one day a sick man was found lying on a mattress inside the gate of this Parsonage. The man admitted that he had been brought there by certain parties, who shall be nameless. "I asked him," said the Bishop, "why had they brought him to my house, and clandestinely, too? 'Oh,' he said, 'They thought you were the proper man' and I suppose I was under the circumstances." So the parsonage became the first hospital in the colony. The Bishop continued: "I appealed to His Excellency, the Governor, who took the matter up and nominated a Provisional Committee as follows: Mr. Dallas, a director of the Hudson's Bay Company, Mr. A. F. Pemberton, Magistrate and Commissioner of Police, and myself, District Minister of Victoria. We used, temporarily a cottage loaned (rent-free) by Mr. Blinkhorn, on the corner of Yates and Broad Street, afterwards occupied by the B.C. Hardware Company, and now by the J. M. Whitney Company, Jewellers. Mr. and Mrs. W. S. Seeley were put in charge, the latter as steward, while a man of Spanish extraction named Emmanuel, faithful, industrious, was 'man of all work,' a title which in those days was not a misnomer."

As the necessity for more accommodation in the new hospital became urgent, the Committee was enlarged and set to work to secure a suitable site for a building. Finally, after much difficulty and discussion, "they took possession of" a piece of land on the Indian reserve and erected a wooden building on the site of what was later to become the Marine Hospital. "The Government, be it noted, though not consulted, offered no objection."

In the following year, 1863, a provision was made for accommodation of female patients and an infirmary for women was established. The Mayoress of Victoria, Mrs. Harris, laid the foundation stone on November 23, 1864. On completion of the infirmary, a letter was received as follows:

My Dear Sir:

I am authorized on behalf of the surgeons attending the "Royal Hospital" to offer the services gratuitously to the Female Hospital.

Will you be so kind as to place this communication before the Director at your earliest convenience.

I am, dear Sir,

Faithfully yours,

James Dixon, M.D.

As hospitals in those days were used only by the poor and indigent, this gratuitous offer was promptly accepted.

An item that appeared in the April 26, 1871, issue of the *British Colonist* seems to indicate the growing concern of the citizens of Victoria for the sick and hurt. It recommended that "the firing of guns by steamships on arrival at or departure from this harbour has been found to have an injurious effect upon the patients of the Royal Hospital, and we are requested to ask a discontinuance. We are sure that the simple request will have the desired effect."

A possible cause for the establishment of a women's hospital at that time is supplied by the historian B. A. McKelvie's story of some curious recent arrivals in the area. About the year 1858, it appears, Victoria was a booming settlement, but the vast predominance of its population was male. Naturally enough, the local stalwarts were very lonesome for female companionship and, to satisfy their need, a ship named *The Seaman's Bride* set out from Australia with a dozen potential brides aboard. On putting in at the brawling city of San Francisco, the girls were promptly carried off and married by the equally lonesome local gallants, who had heard rumours of their presence in town. A second ship, *Tynemouth*, from England, carrying sixty girls and complete with a matronly chaperone, managed to dodge the piratic southerners and arrived safely at Victoria. As the girls were being taken off to the accommodation arranged for them by the Rev. Cridge and his committee, the eager men crowded round. It was not long before the first girl, walking demurely up from the dock, received a courteous and honourable proposal of marriage from a citizen of Sooke. She promptly accepted, and the others soon followed suit. The need for an adequate lying-in facility must have followed in due course.

The practice of medicine in those days had many and varied responsibilities, even as it has today. For example, Dr. Helmcken, on one occasion, was faced with the problem of what treatment should be rendered when Governor Musgrave suffered a compound fracture of his leg. The problem was aggravated by the fact that wound infection, followed by secondary osteomyelitis, was almost inevitable with such injuries and usually resulted in a prolonged convalescence and a crippling disability. It would appear that like the shaman before him, Dr. Helmcken was jealous of his reputation and was wary of accepting the total responsibility for any poor result that might ensue. He prudently allowed his colleagues to dictate treatment, contenting himself with the role of family physician and anaesthetist. Dr. Helmcken's description of the occasion also hints at some overtones of medical rivalry:[5]

At this time Governor Musgrave in getting on his horse, broke his leg — a compound fracture about the ankle, the upper fragment of the tibia protruding. I think I was first to see him, but Powell, Ash and other doctors soon arrived. I did not want the case, and so Powell stepped in somehow or other. I gave the Governor Chloroform and after some trouble Powell and some others got the bones into pretty good apposition. Ash was sulky and grumpy — I think I ought to have proposed him, but Powell had come in earlier.

At this time the antiseptic treatment by means of Carbolic Acid had come in and from Edinburgh had come reports of most extraordinary successes. I did not propose or oppose the treatment. I knew too little of it to do either. Powell however determined to use it — according to what he had read. So the wound was covered with Carbolic Oil and Lint etc. bandaged and there the thing ought to have rested. (blank in ms.) undertook to watch Musgrave during the night, but having the carbolic oil at hand, he thought he ought to apply it frequently — and so he did liberally. There was some misunderstanding about this. Anyhow the treatment was very disappointing — made things worse instead of better, the wound and bones did not go on favourably — the Governor lay in his bed for weeks — and was crippled for life. This probably would have happened under any treatment — for a portion of the tibia died.

Perhaps the most interesting part of the story is the fact that carbolic acid compresses were used at all, even though they were used incorrectly with unfortunate results. At that time, the use of the antiseptic carbolic acid to prevent and combat infection was in its infancy. Lister had published his epoch-making paper, "On the Antiseptic Principle in the Practice of Surgery," only two years prior to Governor Musgrave's accident in a country that still lay six months or more away by sail.

The practice of surgery was a rough and ready one in those days and all physicians were expected to perform with the knife. There were no hospitals as the twentieth century knows them, no resuscitative measures such as blood transfusions or oxygen; there were no air-conditioned operating rooms staffed by highly-trained personnel, no trained assistants, no batteries of electric lights to show up the operative field; there were no absorbable sutures that had been safely sterilized at high temperature; there were no Teflon arterial grafts, nor tantalum prostheses to replace damaged bone. The success of the operation depended entirely upon the trained intelligence, the quick judgment and the nimble fingers of the frontier surgeon. It was his responsibility to supply the instruments he would need, the ligatures that were to be used, the simple sterilizers for boiling the instruments, the iodine to paint the skin and the ether or chloroform to provide the anaesthetic. All too often he worked without an assistant, inducing the anaesthetic himself and handing it over to a nurse or even a neighbour woman to administer under his supervision. He would shave the skin and paint it with iodine, and drape the field of operation with protective clean towels and sheets. He then washed his hands and, if rubber gloves were available, he put them on. If not, he operated without them. He wore no gown, simply rolling up his sleeves and putting on an apron to protect his clothes. A cap to prevent his hair falling into the wound and a mask to prevent infection from his nose and throat were added late in the century.

It was not until 1891 that the first truly experienced surgeon came to British Columbia. Dr. R. E. McKechnie, the author's uncle, arrived bearing credentials of surgical practice in Montreal and elsewhere that prepared him for a noteworthy surgical career in Nanaimo and then in Vancouver. Dr. O. M. Jones, another experienced surgeon, came to Victoria in 1892, and was soon followed by others. But it was, first and foremost, the doctor-patient relationship that became the 19th-century physicians' gift of excellence to the twentieth century. It was epitomized by the affection the people of the province felt for John Sebastian Helmcken, family doctor, who casually carried his stethoscope coiled in his flat derby hat and had a horse by the name of Julia that was known to everyone.

In our own time, dependent as we are on modern methods of communication, rapid transit, health care schemes and other impersonal conveniences, it may be difficult to fathom why and how such a relationship developed. Fortunately, one of Dr. Helmcken's devoted patients, famous for her paintings of British Columbia scenes and Indian life, also had command of a colourful and vivid prose. She was Emily Carr, and she sets down her memories of the good doctor during her childhood in the Victoria of the 1880's:[6]

When Victoria was young specialists had not been invented — the Family Doctor did you all over. You did not have a special doctor for each part. Doctor Helmcken attended to all our ailments — Father's gout, our stomach aches, he even told us what to do once when the cat had fits. If he was wanted in a hurry he got there in no time and did not wait for you to become sicker so that he could make a bigger cure. You began to get better the moment you heard Doctor Helmcken coming up the stairs. He did have the most horrible medicines — castor oil, Gregory's Powder, blue pills, black draughts, sulphur and treacle.

Jokey people called him Doctor Heal-my-Skin. He had been doctor in the old Fort and knew everybody in Victoria. He was very thin, very active, very cheery, he had an old brown mare called Julia. When the doctor came to see Mother we fed Julia at the gate with clover. The doctor loved old Julia. One stormy night he was sent for because Mother was very ill. He came very quickly and Mother said, "I am sorry to bring you and Julia out on such a night, doctor." "Julia is in her stable. What was the good of two of us getting wet?" My little brother fell across a picket fence once and tore his leg. The doctor put him on our dining room sofa and sewed it up. The China boy came rushing in to say, "house all burn up!" Doctor Helmcken put in the last stitch, wiped his needle on his coat sleeve and put it into his case, then stripping off his coat, rushed to the kitchen pump and pumped until the fire was put out.

Once I knelt on a needle which broke into my knee. While I was telling Mother about it who should come up the steps but the doctor! He had just looked in to see the baby who had not been very well. They put me on the kitchen table. The doctor cut slits in my knee and wiggled his fingers around inside for three hours hunting for the piece of needle. They did not know the way of drawing this out with a magnet then, nor did they give chloroform for little things like that.

The doctor said, "Yell, lassie, yell! it will let the pain out." I did yell, but the pain stayed in.

I remember the doctor's glad voice as he said "thank God, I have got all of it now, or the lassie would have been lame for life with that under her knee cap!" Then he washed his hands under the kitchen tap and gave me a peppermint.

Doctor Helmcken knew each part of every one of us. He could have taken us to pieces and put us together again without mixing up any of our legs or our noses or anything.

Doctor Helmcken's office was a tiny two roomed cottage on the lower end of Fort Street near Wharf Street. It sat on a hummocky field; you walked along two planks and came to three steps at the door. The outer room had a big table in the centre filled with bottles of all sizes and shapes. All were empty and all dusty. Round the walls of the room were shelves with more bottles, all full and lots of musty old books. The inner office had a stove that was very higgledy-piggledy. He would allow no one to go in and tidy it up.

The Doctor sat in a round-backed wooden chair before a table; there were three kitchen chairs against the wall for invalid's. He took you over to a very dirty, uncurtained window, jerked up the blind and said "tongue!" then he poked about the middle so hard that things fell out of your pockets. He put a wooden trumpet bang down on your chest and stuck his ear to the other end. After listening and grunting he went into the bottle room, took a bottle, blew the dust off it and emptied out the dead flies. Then he went to the shelves and filled it from several other bottles, corked it, gave it to Mother and sent you home to get well on it. He stood on the step and lit a new cigar after every patient as if he was burning up your symptoms to make room for the next sick person.

PART FOUR

The 20th Century

21

The Environment of Prosperity

As the twentieth century opened, coastal British Columbia had become a land of promise to those fleeing from the poverty and crowding of European cities and countrysides. Here lay a prosperous outpost of empire, governed by the British parliamentary system and regulated by the tenets of British common law. Immigrants were welcome. Land was easily acquired, and would provide a good living for a man and his family if he applied ordinary hard work and diligence to it. The fable of a Northwest Passage had finally become a reality in the form of a transcontinental railway and the province, straddling its western terminus and host to ships bearing the wealth of the Orient, looked forward to a prosperous future.

Such prospects attracted many settlers, both rich and poor, and the region developed rapidly. Because of its association with the British Empire, the area was most attractive and accessible to newcomers from Great Britain and a distinctly English flavour predominated. All arable land within easy access was soon claimed and many of the farms carved out are still under cultivation.

Settlers with money established more traditional types of estates with stately homes and all the graces of fine furnishings, paintings and formal gardens. Fresh food was plentiful and the standard of living was high. Delicacies not available locally could be ordered from London, to be dispatched by responsible shops long experienced in sending such supplies to a far-flung empire. Pantry shelves were filled with English jams, oriental spices and other such delights and the cellars stocked with French wines and champagnes and barrels of eastern Blue-Point oysters shipped from the Maritimes.

In the cities, living conditions were improving steadily. Electricity was becoming available, to be burned as a source of light in glowing carbon-filament lamps suspended from the ceiling by twisted yellow wires. Coal-oil lamps, however, remained in common use. Even those homes wired and socketed for the magic Edison bulbs kept a reserve supply of kerosene and lamps available, for power failures were common and sometimes of long duration — the result often of a wind-blown tree falling across the wires as they carried their quirky cargo through the forests. Along with electric light, there was a new kind of transportation provided by the electric trams and the new-fangled horseless carriage was showing signs of being accepted even by the horse, who less frequently reared and plunged and ran wildly away when the monster put-putted past him. The English-type postal system provided a reliable means of communication and the telephone, though in its infancy, was maturing rapidly, doctors and pharmacists now being expected to have telephones in their homes. Even more important, perhaps, was the worldwide telegraphic network that permitted the outpost province to keep in touch with events of significance everywhere.

To add to the creature comforts, most homes were heated by stoves and fireplaces, and wood was available for the gathering. Ice, delivered by horse-drawn wagons, served as a refrigerant. Oriental servants were available at a cost varying from ten to twenty-five dollars a month. It was, for the more fortunate, a life of material ease unprecedented in the annals of ordinary men. Through it all, the majority of the residents, English-born or descended, maintained a fierce loyalty to their heritage. When the Royal Navy sent ships "to show the Flag" it was a gala event and Victoria and Vancouver turned out in force. All in all, the citizen of British Columbia led a proud and contented life. He respected his King and worshipped his God and put his trust in the strength of the Royal Navy.

22

Hygiene and Diet

IT WAS A COUNTRY filled with rugged individualists, believers in
the customs that have endured the ages. Thus, the doctors'
attempts to introduce proper hygienic habits and sanitation met
with varying success.

Many of the pioneers were transients who lived in crude, split-
cedar shacks in the forest, in home-made float houses moored
along the salt-chuck, or in dirty white tents pitched on any vacant
spot of land. The great outdoors had been and still was their disposal unit and they were not concerned with modern sanitary
procedures. Given time, they were sure, nature would take care of
the problems of pollution.

In the minds of officials, the adult population represented an
almost insurmountable sanitary and hygienic problem. Thus, a
long-range health programme was developed that was aimed primarily at the future citizens of British Columbia — the school
children.

General standards of cleanliness were so low in many homes
that, at the beginning of each school term, it was an important
part of the opening exercises for each teacher to inspect her
charges with great care as to their cleanliness and their general
state of health. The children were examined for signs of body-lice,
ringworm, scabies, and the commonplace nits of the hair. A remarkable number were found to require attention, and these were

taken to the school nurse for follow-up care. Throughout the winter months, the teacher continued to make periodic inspections, looking for children suffering from that common but painful complaint, chilblains, or any sign of such communicable diseases as mumps, chicken pox, smallpox, scarlet fever or tuberculosis.

The school doctor, in his turn, examined each child once a year and was on the lookout for dental caries, deficiency states (such as rickets), infected tonsils and adenoids, undetected heart lesions and other less obvious conditions. These examinations were quite frequently the first the young child had ever had.

Daily physical drill was held to build up the bodies of the coming generation, and periodic lectures on the principles of health and hygiene were given in the school. Fresh air was a fetish, possibly because of the prevalence of tuberculosis and the belief that large doses of fresh air would tend to prevent it. All children were instructed to sleep with their windows wide open top and bottom to allow for proper circulation.

It was stressed that this be done in winter as well as summer. As a result, bedrooms tended to be cold and even flannelette sheets were found none too warm by bare feet. It became the habit of many a child and even some adults to undress at record speed, leaving their warm underwear on under their night clothes. They would then jump quickly into bed, pulling the bed covers over their heads to conserve the heat of their breath, and lie shivering while they waited for the bed to warm up. Only then would they stick their noses out from beneath the covers.

The pinched blue faces and the frequency of chronic nasopharyngeal congestion made little impression on the vigorous surviving adults. They continued to insist that the cold, fresh air was "healthy." Until recently, many of the boarding schools of the "Old Country" type continued to preach the necessity of cold bedrooms and cold fresh air "to make a man" out of some undernourished youngster who needed, above all, warmth and comfort, in addition to good food.

Many adults instituted their own personal hygiene and physical fitness programmes. In those days, enough hot water for a bath was only available in most homes after vigorous and prolonged stoking of the kitchen stove. A daily hot bath was thus difficult to come by. In consequence, it became the custom of many families to fire up the kitchen stove on Saturdays, bake and cook for the coming Sabbath, and to make Saturday the night of the bath for the whole family. As many homes had not progressed to indoor plumbing, it was often necessary to use a portable bathtub. The family gathered in the warm kitchen and the tub was filled with hot water. Mother went first as she was considered to be the cleanest. She soaped herself all over with a bar of hard, yellow castile soap, often home-made from wood ashes and fat dripping. Father came second to the tub, and more hot water was added as needed. The rest followed in turn, and the order of the bath became a vital instrument of privilege in a large family, akin to the "pecking order" of today. When all were clean and dressed in their nightclothes and ready for bed, it was time for cocoa and cookies and a bedtime story. Family ties were never closer.

Others who worshipped at the "Temple of Hygiea" took a cold bath each morning. It was a commendable effort in those days when the twice-yearly bath was still a commonplace. As the houses were underheated by today's standards, the restoration of the body heat after the cold plunge was best accomplished by an energetic towelling with a rough "Turkish" towel and a marked increase of body activity to produce the needed calories of heat. A vigorous four- or five-mile walk around Vancouver's Stanley Park in fair weather and foul, followed by a good breakfast and a quick tramp of a mile or so to the office completed the revitalizing of the frigidly cleansed individual. Of course, this sudden immersion in cold water produced its share of casualties, but these were passed off by the dedicated as part of nature's programme for the survival of the fittest.

Because of the poorly heated homes, heavy clothing was worn indoors and out. Wool from Scotland was the favourite, as the Scots had long since perfected the art of blending wool and whiskey to keep them warm in their cold, damp climate. Beneath the tweeds, men, women and children wore the standard "Long John" underwear that covered them from the neck to ankle and offered an ingenious "trap door" built into the seat, for minimum exposure during the exercise of normal bodily functions. There was an endless row of buttons down the front, however, and these had a tendency to succumb to the occasional roughness of young fingers. In an effort to solve this problem many children were sewn into their underwear in the fall and taken out only in the springtime.

With food aplenty in field, forest, river and sea, there was no problem of starvation. Indeed, the problem was one that runs contrary to today's dietary beliefs. In addition to making sure of an adequate intake of food to fuel the daily work requirements, it was desirable to maintain a thick layer of adipose tissue as a thermal blanket in the cool of the temperate climate. Men engaged in logging or other heavy outdoor work where labour-saving devices were practically unknown required a food intake of about 4,000 or 5,000 calories per day. Even the energy output associated with ordinary day-to-day chores was more demanding of calories than is the case today. In addition, there was the problem of caloric heat loss through radiation into the cool surrounding atmosphere.

These conditions existed in a society where obesity was no disgrace. As a result, the meals that were served were heavy — rich in cream, butter, fresh farm eggs, thick slices of home-made bread, roast meats with gravies and pie crusts made with the purest of lards. Eating was considered not only a necessity, but a pleasure and a sport. Any man who could tuck away great quantities of food was respected and admired for his capacity, and his post-prandial rumbles were listened for and welcomed by the cook, who interpreted them as the sincerest form of appreciation. Such adulation inevitably led to rivalry and eating contests became the vogue. One of the last of these recorded took place in Vancouver shortly before World War I, when two old-timers went into Leonard's Cafe on Pender Street and each politely ordered a stack of hot cakes, two fried eggs with thick slices of bacon, buttered toast and coffee. To the young, inexperienced waitress, this was a normal order and she filled it pleasantly. A second order from each of the contestants was rather more puzzling and, when they requested a third order of the "same," she began to suspect that she was dealing with a couple of madmen and sent for the manager. On his arrival, he quickly took in the situation and reassured the startled girl who continued to serve the two men, growing steadily more dazed by the amount they ate. The winner ate two dozen eggs, with all the bacon, hot cakes, toast and coffee that went with them. Modern-day nutritionists would have shuddered with revulsion.

23

A Doctor's Life

IN ADDITION TO THE FAMILY DOCTOR, the late nineteenth century produced scientific discoveries that were to change the whole concept of medical care. Pasteur had given the world a science of bacteriology that altered the concept of the etiology and spread of disease. T. G. Morton had produced that great boon to surgery, ether, a safe general anaesthetic. Lister had progressively worked his technical way from the "crude German creosote" compresses to the antiseptic carbolic spray, and ended with the accepted technique of asepsis. Roentgen had discovered a technique for taking films of broken bones and other tissues. Billroth had worked out the surgical techniques of partial gastrectomy. Halstead had described his superbly detailed dissection for removal of a cancerous breast, based on his pathological studies. Haematology and blood chemistry were in their infancy, but had started on their long and important journeys of discovery, and the value and usefulness of the hypodermic needle and syringe for the administration of controlled dosages of drugs had been established.

For all the new diagnostic and therapeutic techniques that were coming to the doctor's aid, many citizens of the time continued, when in trouble, to place most of their faith in religious teachings. Doubtlessly, when illness was severe or pain acute, a bit of aid from a more secular source was appreciated. But such aid was sought reluctantly. The very real fear of the physicians drastic pukes and purges, the surgeon's painful cuttings and probings, proved hard to overcome.

As more and more stories of modern medical miracles made the rounds, however, the physician found his practice growing in size, as well as in complexity. His was a busy life, full of bustle and motion, not all of it medical.

Socially, the doctor and his wife were expected to grace with their presence any event that was at all out of the ordinary. When Caruso or Madame Melba gave their concerts or Pavlova danced, the doctor dressed in his formal white tie and tails and, accompanied by his faultlessly gowned wife, attended the dinners that preceded the theatre, or the oyster suppers that followed them.

The doctor still gave little thought to his fees. There was not much money in circulation, and most of his patients had little, or none at all. Furthermore, money was considered a material matter that had no place in the almost spiritual relationship that existed between physician and patient. When the doctor did send a bill to a patient who could well afford his fee, it was customary for the patient to leave it unobtrusively in an envelope on the corner of the doctor's desk, after what was apparently a purely social visit.

The doctor, however, was rewarded in other ways. Grateful patients made a point of supplying him and his family with the necessities of life. Sacks of potatoes and other vegetables arrived on his doorstep, in season. Fruit came by the crate, and the doctor's wife was kept busy making jams and jellies and other preserves for the winter. With the advent of the hunting season came braces of duck and pheasant from the Fraser River Delta and the interior. There were hindquarters of venison and beef or lamb. Patients who had nothing to give showed their respect in other ways. A doctor rarely received a ticket for a traffic violation or other minor offence. He was known to the constables and invariably the remark was, "I'm sorry, doctor. I didn't know it was you." The author's father, Dr. William C. McKechnie, received a salute each time he drove past the walrus-moustached pointsman on duty at the corner of Hastings and Granville Streets, and it was noted by his family that somehow his route invariably took him by there when he had visitors from out-of-town in his shiny brass-bound Overland car.

At the hospital, the doctor was waited on hand and foot, and made welcome to the best the cook had to offer at any time of day or night. There was no charge for hitching his horse and buggy to the hospital hitching post. If the nurses wanted to know whether a certain doctor was in the hospital, they looked out the window to see if his hitching post was occupied. Dr. Stuart Ross always rode a big white horse and Dr. R. E. McKechnie had his own coach, complete with coachman.

The doctor worked long and hard. In return, he lived a life of dignity and respect. He could afford the worldly comforts and even some of the luxuries. Soon, however, such a life would no longer be possible without a substantial money income. Nor would a doctor be able to provide his patients with up-to-date care without a sizable investment in education, equipment and facilities. Inevitably, the doctor's relationship to some of the tenets in the Hippocratic creed would change.

THE OATH OF HIPPOCRATES ✍

I SWEAR BY APOLLO PHYSICIAN, BY ÆSCULAPIUS, BY HEALTH, BY PANACEA AND BY ALL THE GODS AND GODDESSES, MAKING THEM MY WITNESSES, THAT I WILL CARRY OUT, ACCORDING TO MY ABILITY AND JUDGMENT, THIS OATH AND THIS INDENTURE. TO HOLD MY TEACHER IN THIS ART EQUAL TO MY OWN PARENTS; TO MAKE HIM PARTNER IN MY LIVELIHOOD, WHEN HE IS IN NEED OF MONEY TO SHARE MINE WITH HIM; TO CONSIDER HIS FAMILY AS MY OWN BROTHERS, AND TO TEACH THEM THIS ART, IF THEY WANT TO LEARN IT, WITHOUT FEE OR INDENTURE; TO IMPART PRECEPT, ORAL INSTRUCTION, AND ALL OTHER INSTRUCTION TO MY OWN SONS, THE SONS OF MY TEACHER, AND TO INDENTURED PUPILS WHO HAVE TAKEN THE PHYSICIAN'S OATH, BUT TO NOBODY ELSE. I WILL USE TREATMENT TO HELP THE SICK ACCORDING TO MY ABILITY AND JUDGMENT, BUT NEVER WITH A VIEW TO INJURY AND WRONG-DOING. NEITHER WILL I ADMINISTER A POISON TO ANYBODY WHEN ASKED TO DO SO, NOR WILL I SUGGEST SUCH A COURSE. SIMILARLY I WILL NOT GIVE TO A WOMAN A PESSARY TO CAUSE ABORTION. BUT I WILL KEEP PURE AND HOLY BOTH MY LIFE AND MY ART. I WILL NOT USE THE KNIFE, NOT EVEN, VERILY, ON SUFFERERS FROM STONE, BUT I WILL GIVE PLACE TO SUCH AS ARE CRAFTSMEN THEREIN. INTO WHATSOEVER HOUSES I ENTER, I WILL ENTER TO HELP THE SICK, AND I WILL ABSTAIN FROM ALL INTENTIONAL WRONG-DOING AND HARM, ESPECIALLY FROM ABUSING THE BODIES OF MAN OR WOMAN, BOND OR FREE. AND WHAT-SOEVER I SHALL SEE OR HEAR IN MY INTERCOURSE WITH MEN, IF IT BE WHAT SHOULD NOT BE PUB-LISHED ABROAD, I WILL NEVER DIVULGE, HOLD-ING SUCH THINGS TO BE HOLY SECRETS. NOW IF I CARRY OUT THIS OATH, AND BREAK IT NOT, MAY I GAIN FOR EVER REPUTATION AMONG ALL MEN FOR MY LIFE AND FOR MY ART; BUT IF I TRANSGRESS IT AND FORSWEAR MYSELF, MAY THE OPPOSITE BEFALL ME.

The Patient's Problems

THE PRACTICE OF MEDICINE in pre-World War I days was increasingly enlightened — yet not always as successful as it might have been. The doctor was becoming wiser as the years rolled by, but he was severely handicapped by inadequate facilities to carry out procedures he knew to be effective. The principles involved in the use of metal plates to hold difficult fractures in position were well known, but the metal and screws contained impurities that resulted in electrolysis and loosening of the plates. In cirrhosis of the liver with portal hypertension, Vidal in 1903 went so far as to create an Eck fistula between the obstructed and distended portal vein and the vena cava — an operation known today as a porto-caval shunt. The procedure was surgically successful, but the patient died, presumably as a result of profound biochemical imbalances brought about by his long-standing and advanced cirrhosis. Many other instances could be cited where the skill of the doctor was balked because supporting sciences had not caught up.

In general, however, the patient considered the treatment he received a vast improvement over the medicine of his father's day. As yet, though, he was not fully convinced it was the last word and was inclined when seriously ill to place his faith in the good Lord rather than the good doctor. It was said that he knew little about disease except how to die from it.

In spite of his ignorance, the patient often attempted to treat himself symptomatically, especially if he considered his problem one of the common ailments and pains. In this he was "aided" by an abundant supply of patent medicines available over the counters of the Hudson's Bay Company and other otherwise reputable merchants. Some remedies did provide effective relief for such conditions as the ordinary coughs and colds and stomach upsets. However, many useless preparations were advertised widely as cure-alls, complete with testimonials. As an example:

Doctor Ham's Invigorating Spirit. A new discovery. A delicious beverage to cure bad spirits, dyspepsia, nervousness, heartburn, colic, pains, etcetera. Weak and sickly constitutions are suddenly restored to health and vigor. Persons, who from dissipating too much overnight and feel the evil effects of the poisonous liquors will find one dose will remove all bad feelings. Ladies of weak and sickly constitutions should take the invigorating spirit three times per day; it will make you strong, healthy and happy, remove all the irregularities from the menstrual organs, and restore the bloom of health to shrivelled and wasted care worn faces.

Most of the medicines used as pain killers contained opium or Cannabis Indica and were sold across the counter without prescription. Pure opium itself, or one of its powerful derivatives, could be purchased the same way, and there were many addicts unsuspected even by themselves, like the dear old lady who sought security for her eternal future from the church and her day-to-day euphoria from her little blue bottle of laudanum.

The availability of these narcotics was of no concern to the authorities, as there were no laws at that time controlling their distribution and use. When such laws were first passed, they were instigated by a layman, not a physician. The Honourable H. H. Stevens, after a lifetime of public service looking back at the age of 92 on his youthful days in Vancouver, recounts the tale: About the year 1903, he was in charge of a grocery store that was suffering from pilferage. He found that two of the clerks had been stealing and, on inquiry, they blamed it on gambling debts incurred in Chinatown. Stevens visited these open gambling dens and found that, among other practices, the Chinese were importing balls of crude opium from India, refining it and selling it to the young bloods of the city. Incensed, he published daily articles on what he had witnessed in *The News Advertiser*. This did not stir up enough action to satisfy him, so he contacted the Reverend Doctor S. Dwight Chown, secretary of the Department of Temperance, Prohibition & Moral Reform of the Methodist Church and took him on several personally conducted tours of the opium dens. Doctor Chown, in turn, travelled to Ottawa and reported what he had seen to W. L. MacKenzie King. The latter became concerned about the problem and introduced in Parliament the first narcotics control act in all of Canada. Premier McBride of British Columbia soon followed his lead and narcotics and other drugs had their first legal sanctions.

Stubborn and persistent pain was a major medical problem of the day. Pain seems to breed more pain, building up and eventually destroying the individual's normal and innate courage. Fear of more pain comes to dominate his life, and the strongest man will reach a stage where he will whimper and cry when faced with the prospect of the slightest hurt, though he may know that it is inflicted for his own benefit. So much was this the case, that the afflicted often accepted a painful condition and suffered it in silence rather than seek the even more painful cure offered by the doctor.

Herniae were common and were controlled by a truss, where possible, but they often outgrew the treatment. Surgical repair today is simple, but then it was terrifying and extremely painful. The open-drop ether anaesthetic was unpleasant to take and, when over, left the patient violently ill for days. This was followed by the "gas pains" caused by the painful distension of the gut and retention of wind secondary to the manipulation of the bowel as it was stuffed back into the abdominal cavity. A little touch of low-grade infective peritonitis was suspected in the most severe cases and this added to the patient's troubles. The distention of the gut — caused by ileus — tended to lead, in turn, to urinary retention, necessitating frequent painful catheterization of the urinary bladder and the almost inevitable bladder infection. As it is human nature to exaggerate any story of one's own suffering, word soon spread and those with herniae became more determined to keep them. As they grew older and their abdominal musculature weakened, the hernia became more difficult to control and finally strangulated. A herniotomy, the cutting of the crural ring, was then performed, but all too often the patient died. Small wonder hernia was sometimes termed a killer of old men.

Hemorrhoids or piles — those varicose veins of the rectum — were commonplace. They emerged in great rosettes from the anal orifice and, at times, their unflower-like swelling was larger than a man's fist and had to be stuffed back behind the anal sphincter by hand several times a day. Clean underwear was an impossibility under those circumstances. When inflammation of the mass occurred, the veins thrombosed and the pain was so profound and disturbing that large doses of opiates did little to assuage it. To those who have suffered the problem or have encountered others thus afflicted, it is readily understandable that when Napoleon's piles thrombosed, his mind may not have been entirely on strategy — with possible disastrous consequences for the Battle of Waterloo.

The sympathetic but painful roughness of the doctor, when treating his patient, was another cause of fear. The doctor probed wounds vigorously and correctly when indicated, and the pain was at times quite severe. He practised many a little trick to catch a patient unawares when something painful but necessary was in order. Such a trick was used by Dr. W. C. McKechnie when he wished to open an abscess or a felon on the end of a finger. In those days before antibiotics, local infections were common and were so dangerous, if not opened quickly and relieved of their painful tension, that Dr. McKechnie carried a special knife in his pocket. It looked like an ordinary pocket-knife, but the blade, when opened up, was curved downwards at the end to a sharp point. The technique was to wipe the blade unobtrusively with alcohol or iodine and conceal it in the palm of the hand, blade pointing down under the index finger. The fearful patient with his throbbing digit would gingerly extend his hand to show the sore finger, whereupon the good doctor would grab the wrist firmly and quickly plunge the curved point of the knife into the abscessed cavity. As the patient yelled and pulled his hand away, the incision was extended satisfactorily.

Painful digestive disorders were frequent and "colic" was a common self-diagnosis. Paregoric and other opium derivatives were on every shelf to relieve such pain. When intestinal obstruction occurred, a patient was purged and puked and his lower bowel irritated with a variety of concoctions, such as enemas of milk and molasses, or an emulsion of hot soap suds. Massive hot stoops made with turpentine were placed on the abdomen and, if those measures did not relieve the patient, surgery was available as a last resort.

The pain of gallstone colic was commonplace and severe. Cholecystectomy was performed frequently, but many patients were still suspicious and afraid of surgery. Some of those who refused surgery developed progressive complications and the discharge of gallstones into the intestines or through the abdominal wall was not uncommon. Of those discharged into the gut, some were so large that they caused intestinal obstruction.

As the lower mainland was supplied by fresh mountain water containing few minerals, goitres were so commonplace that the area was considered to be a "goitre belt." Large adenomatous goitres were frequently seen on the street and quite often they eroded the trachea and caused it to collapse, necessitating an emergency operation to prevent the patient's choking to death. It was impossible to raise pigs in the Fraser Valley, as the piglets were born with large colloid goitres that often stopped their breathing. The goitre problem was corrected when the importance of iodine in the diet was recognized.

Ovarian cysts were common among women but it was not considered "cricket" to remove a cyst that was smaller than a grapefruit. Some of the cysts grew so large they occupied the whole of the abdominal cavity, and the patient not only had difficulty breathing but was unable to ingest a satisfactory amount of food. Such cysts were awkward but not impossible to remove, though they often weighed as much as thirty five pounds.

Gonorrhea and syphilis remained more or less commonplace and, at the turn of the century, there was still no specific treatment. To make matters worse, the church, preaching the seventh commandment, invoked the fear of venereal disease as a psychological deterrent. This often led to particularly tragic consequences, as any woman who developed a pelvic infection, usually secondary to the generally poor accouchement procedures of the day, was considered to have venereal disease. No smears or cultures were available, to prove or disprove the possibility. If the woman's virtue was beyond reproach, the poor husband was brow-beaten by the zealous doctor and quizzed about any and every extra-marital connection he may have had in his life. Woe betide the husband who, in his youth, had seduced the hired girl behind the barn! Did not everyone know that venereal disease was insidious and could remain dormant for years? And if the husband believed himself pure, what must he have believed of his innocent wife?

The ordinary source of venereal disease was the prostitute. She customarily took precautions to prevent becoming infected, but these were not always successful and one infected prostitute could infect many men. It was the custom in those days for the liaisons to take place in "houses of pleasure" run by a "madam" who had grown old in the service and who bossed the young women. Prostitution was apparently a recognized profession, as witness the accounts records of St. Paul's Hospital that list "prostitute" as the occupation of the female being admitted.

These "houses of pleasure" served the purpose of providing all forms of entertainment to the loggers and others who came to the city after months of hard work in isolated camps up the coast. When the logger hit town, he was "raring to go" and the first place he headed for was the bar. A few drinks, and he was ready for a bit of female companionship. Greeting him at the door of her "house," the madam purloined his bankroll and detailed one of her girls to look after him and he was royally entertained with wine, women and song. When eventually the money ran out, he was given a ticket back to his camp, a bottle of whiskey to help his hangover, and an invitation to come again the next time he was in town. He had received value for his money and he was content. All too often, however, the signs of venereal disease appeared after he had returned to his isolated camp and, broke and unable to get into town, he had to use the relatively ineffective remedies provided by those he worked for, and so the disease maintained its continuity as in the days of Captain Cook.[1]

Larger coastal establishments, realizing that men sometimes needed female companionship and the solace of liquor, permitted responsible madams to maintain their houses nearby. These went under such descriptive names as "Poison Flats" or "Pecker Point" and it was the responsibility of the madam to keep her girls "clean" and to see to it that the men were sober when they went on shift the next day.

Early in the century, the value of intravenous arsenical preparations in combating syphilis was discovered. As the technique of intravenous therapy was not well established, many a sloughing wound resulted from the leakage of the irritating arsenicals from the vein into the subcutaneous tissues. The average course of treatment in an uncomplicated case covered a two year period, but even so was not always effective. Many a patient went on to the tertiary stages of syphilis, blissfully ignorant that he had not been cured by the long period of expensive and, at times, painful therapy.

One of the earliest anti-syphilitic arsenicals came from Germany and was known as Compound No. 606, or just plain 606. It was a wonder drug of its time and the significance of the figures was known to everybody. As a result, a drug store in the Vancouver Block was proud of its astuteness when it obtained the telephone number 606, in those days of operator-switched service and a single exchange.

About the same time, silver compounds such as argyrol were found to be useful in the treatment of gonorrhea. The urethra was injected full of the compound and kept that way for several minutes at least twice a day and these indignities had to be suffered for a minimum of three months.

Argyrol was also considered a wonder drug in its day, being used not only for gonorrhea but for the then prevalent chronic nasopharyngeal and eye infections. Some patients took it on themselves to put a few drops of the argyrol in their eyes or nose every day.

After a few years, this led to a characteristic blue-gray discolouration of the skin and the "moons" of their nail-beds, the result of the silver being absorbed into their bodies and retained by the reticulo-endothelial system. There were a number of such recognizable cases walking the streets and the last known one died in Vancouver in 1968.

The problem of unwanted pregnancy was as frequent then as it is today. Abortion laws were rigid and the ethics of church and medical profession were adamant. Nonetheless, women who were in the family way had their remedies, if they were desperate enough. Among the new doctors arriving in British Columbia were some who had been sent to the limbo of the "colonies" because they had disgraced their family at home. These were known as "remittance men," owing to the regular allowances sent them by their families to keep them from the ancestral doorstep. At least one of these, an enterprising Englishman, was reputed to have made a small fortune by taking his patients on a short sea voyage out of Victoria to the International Boundary Line in the Straits of Juan de Fuca. While lying on this boundary line, he performed the desired operation. If an American patrol boat appeared, he would move over into Canadian waters. A Canadian ship would send him on a reverse course.[2]

Another scheming doctor anticipated modern medicine by importing what was known as an "Abrams Machine." This machine was a very "scientific" one and the gullible public, with their neo-scientific orientation, fell hard for it. The principle was that some of the body fluids were sent to the doctor along with the requisite fee. The machine analyzed the fluid and sent back a report telling the patient what was the matter with him and what should be done. Legally, it was a marginal operation and difficult to stop. It was said that, finally, some members of the Vancouver Medical Association sent a sample to be tested under a woman's name. They received a report describing her menstrual problems and the fact that she might even be pregnant. When they sent a scathing letter to the operator naming a male doctor as the sample's donor, he answered insisting he had known who it was all the time and was just going along with the gag.

In reality, he stated, the sample indicated an individual in the advanced stages of syphilis. This shut the doctors up. In that age of over-the-fence gossip, such an insinuation could seriously damage a doctor's reputation.

Smallpox, one of the white man's deadly gifts to the Indian, remained a dangerous problem. Although vaccine was available and the Hudson's Bay Company saw to it that as many Indians as possible were vaccinated, it persisted stubbornly. The white man himself remained the major source of infection, due largely to the so-called "conscientious objectors" who refused vaccination on grounds of religious or other bias. As a result, frequent epidemics of smallpox swept through the whole of British Columbia. Few doctors practising today have seen an epidemic, but those who have will never forget it. Individual pustules broke out on the body, the number depending on the virulence of the disease and the resistance of the individual. Sometimes the whole body was almost completely covered. Even the eyes could be affected. The pustules often joined together and became confluent, and the purulent discharge had a dread, unpleasant odour. The disease was very toxic to the patient, who lay there somnolent, waiting for it to take its course. Those who survived were permanently marked as each pustule destroyed a circular area in the skin and left its characteristic, readily recognized pitted scar. When the infection affected the cornea of the eye, the resultant scar tissue often destroyed sight in that eye.

Typhoid fever also is rare today and many practising physicians have not seen a patient with the disease. This speaks well for the activities of the public health authorities, as typhoid is a disease of contamination, and the coastal cities had more than their share of epidemics. The patient typically went into a deep coma that was known as a "typhoid state." A remittant daily temperature reached as high as 106°F. at times. With that high a fever the patient very often was delirious, and pandemonium reigned in an open ward full of such cases. It was the practice in some hospitals to plunge delirious patients with high fever into a tub of water, filled with ice to ensure its coldness. The fever usually was reduced, but the reaction of the hot and already babbling patient, when first immersed, was spectacular. None but the most blase or busy intern or nurse would miss the event. (The disease has almost disappeared in Canada. The Canadian Army serving in the Boer War had more casualties from typhoid fever than from enemy action. During World War II, typhoid fever was a rarity.)

Measles and "influenza," also introduced by the white man, were lethal diseases for the Indian, who had no natural or acquired immunity to protect him.

A rather unusual side to the practice of medicine in British Columbia concerned the large number of Chinese residents who originally had been brought over by the Canadian Pacific Railway to provide labour battalions during the early construction days. The Chinese men, with their pigtails, their black silk skull caps, blouses and pantaloons, and their English limited to a rattling sing-song dialect of "pidgin-English," were willing workmen. They were readily recruited, transported cheaply across the Pacific in C.P.R. ships and, once landed, they required only the simplest living accommodations. Their diet consisted of large volumes of rice, with occasional small bits of meat and fresh vegetables. When the railway was completed many of them elected to remain, coalescing into colonies in Victoria, Vancouver and elsewhere. There were no Chinese women and the men lived together in rooms lined with tiers of partially enclosed bunks that could be completely closed off by curtains. Ventilation was poor and the air carried an aromatic burden blended of body odours, the smell of food, the pungent emanations of punk sticks, with a frequent overlay of opium fumes.

Resistance to disease was minimal and tuberculosis was rampant. When taken to the hospital, the men were adamant in their refusal to permit any operation. Whether an operation was indicated or not, they almost invariably faded away and died. It seemed not to matter what was wrong with them. These mysterious deaths, often contrary to every reasonable prognosis, led to the spread of the legend that the men were committing ritual suicide by taking a mysterious "black pill."

It was not until after World War II that the mystery was

finally cleared up. The men apparently believed that they went through eternity the way they left this world. Understandably, they did not want anything removed from them prior to their demise. Their apparent mysterious dissolution in the face of treatment was primarily a result of nutritional deficiencies. They were what one investigator called "rice burners," with little else to augment their diet, and their body was in a constant state of nutritional deficit. When autopsied, many of the men were found to have a mysterious ailment that, for want of a better name, was called primary cancer of the liver. In reality, it was probably a result of this dietary deficiency.

When a Chinaman died, he was given an opulent funeral by his tong amid pomp and ceremony. All the little white boys of the neighbourhood gathered around the burial ground, for it was the Chinese custom to pile the grave high with flowers and sweets, candied fruit and ginger and, for the wealthier deceased, even a roast pig. At the end of a five year interval, the pelvic and thigh bones and certain other bones of the departed were dug up, sealed in cans and shipped back to the home of their ancestors. The event was duly noted in the newspapers of the day.

With the importation of so many Chinese labourers, it was inevitable that some Oriental diseases would be imported also. Leprosy was one of these. Its incubation period extended over many years and many of the workers were infected when they arrived. The Chinese themselves dreaded the disease and it was reported on April 1, 1882, that one Ah Kye, a leprous Chinese resident of New Westminster, was found hanged and his body partially burned, presumably by fellow countrymen anxious to prevent contagion. Leprosy became common enough to cause the provincial government to establish a leprosarium on D'Arcy Island in 1892. Later, the federal government took it over and moved the facility to Bentinck Island. As care improved, the number of lepers diminished and the leprosarium was finally closed in the late 1920's.[3]

India was another source of Oriental immigrants to Vancouver, but they created few medical problems. When one of them died, a funeral pyre was built on the sand of the old Kitsilano Indian

Reserve at the mouth of False Creek and the body was cremated. The ashes were thrown into the Pacific Ocean, to mingle with the infinitesimal amounts of water it contained from the sacred Ganges River of India. One of the last such ceremonies took place in 1942.

Among the white population, it was customary at the turn of the century to have large families. The infant mortality rate was high and every family could expect one or more deaths among the children. According to the law of averages, they were liable also to have a child who was mentally deficient, deaf, dumb or blind. Such children were accepted with resignation and taken care of openly by the rest of the family. So widespread were these disabilities that the Dominion Bureau of Statistics found it necessary, during census taking, to inquire about the presence in the home of people who were deaf and dumb, blind, or of unsound mind. The rest of the children were expected to be reasonably healthy and to take care of their parents during their old age, in the absence of any form of government pension.

With the rapid advance of medical science, the practising doctor had difficulty keeping up with new discoveries. One common medium for professional self-improvement was the textbook, and many excellent volumes were published. As most doctors graduated from medical school with little if any surgical or obstetrical training, some of the textbooks produced on the subject were so practical and so explicit that a modern internist, inexperienced with scalpel, admitted that even he could do surgery, if he but followed the instructions diligently. A practical knowledge of human anatomy was desirable and physicians had recourse to an 1869 ordinance "restricting the practice of surgery and for the encouragement of the study of anatomy." It dealt with unclaimed bodies, and entitled any qualified medical practitioner to secure a body for dissection. Section 9 required a personal security of one hundred dollars and two additional securities of fifty dollars each, so that a decent interment would be given the bodies after they had served their purpose.

In the early 1900's, Doctor Henry Esson Young, Provincial Secretary in the McBride government, inaugurated a farsighted policy dealing with mental illnesses that was capable of uniform expansion, to provide for the needs of future generations. Much of his organizational structure is still functioning today. A little later, as Minister of Education, he launched the provincial university. He secured an endowment of two million acres of public lands — to include the splendid, scenic site at Point Grey where the present university stands — and a grant of $2,500,000 for initiating the undertaking. A medical doctor, Frank Wesbrook, was chosen as president. From the first, a medical faculty was planned, to be inaugurated as soon as the university was firmly established. Construction had begun and the concrete skeleton of the science building had been poured when World War I intervened and further development of the university was postponed until the post-war period. Even then, progress was slow, and it was not until after World War II that it began to accelerate. Finally, in 1954, the first class of young doctors graduated from the university.

25

War and Money

THE WAR THAT BROKE OUT BETWEEN England and Germany in
1914 hit hard at far-off British Columbia. The predominantly
English population immediately packed up in large numbers and
left for England to join the Armed Forces. Many of them never
returned, and their farms and establishments went to rack and
ruin. Other British Columbians joined the Canadian Armed
Forces, and of these the doctors were among the foremost. Most
of those remaining were old or had some physical defect, but
this usually did not prevent them from working overtime to take
care of their augmented case loads. In addition, many found time
to drill in the local militia, because, in the early days of the war,
it was anticipated that Victoria and Vancouver might fall to the
German fleet. The cities did not succumb and, eventually, the
training was lessened.

As the war drew to a close, the tired civilian doctors were faced
with another problem. This was the great Spanish influenza
epidemic that swept through the world and took so many lives.
British Columbia was no exception and, although stringent preventative measures were instituted, these proved of little value. An
immunizing serum was developed, but it was neither readily
available nor sufficiently effective. Whole families were wiped out
and many children orphaned. Schools were closed and public
gatherings were forbidden. Small towns took their own special

measures to protect themselves. The coastal town of Powell River, for instance, had a doctor meet and examine every passenger who wished to disembark from the Union Steamship boat. If there was no evidence of the early stages of "flu" the visitor was given a small surgical-type mask to cover his mouth and nose, and asked to wear it continuously. It was difficult to be certain that such measures were effective but, in general, the citizens of the town felt psychologically more secure.

The disease was a virulent one. It struck rapidly and the patients developed a toxic, congestive pneumonia that, because of its appearance at autopsy, was termed a "black pneumonia." Faces became flushed with a peculiar type of cyanosis that, because of its unusual colour, was known as "heliotrope cyanosis." Nose-bleeds were common and were so severe that they required the packing of both nasal passages. The hospitals were flooded with patients and it was necessary to build temporary wooden buildings to house the overflow. Due to the sudden onset of the disease, the volume of the work, and the frequency of the nasal haemorrhages, the doctors were on the go day and night, many becoming so seriously exhausted that their acquired immunity was overwhelmed and they themselves succumbed to the influenza and died. Others had to stop work, quite unable to carry on, and it was at this time that some of the few remaining shamans were reported to have taken up their art again among the Indian population in remote areas.

Before the Great War, the doctor-patient relationship had reached an all-time high. Now it began to show signs of a decline, due to the demands on the surviving doctors' time and the drag-down effect of the dollar sign. Canada was struggling to finance her war effort and was searching for new and taxable sources of money. Under that pressure, the income tax was introduced. Though the amounts involved were not large at the start, the hard-pressed doctor was concerned. On inquiry, he was assured that he, as a doctor, did not have to pay, as the tax was designed solely to "soak the rich." However, like its associate in inevitability, death, after three years of exemption, his taxes were to catch up with him and they were collected yearly thereafter. With increasing taxation and other expenses, the doctor became increasingly concerned about money. And his patients, obliged now to fill the doctor's bank account rather than his larder, began to grumble about the tarnished wings of their one-time angels of mercy. The old-time "family doctor," working long hours with money the least of his rewards, was becoming obsolete.

The Roar of the Twenties

THE MEN WHO RETURNED FROM BATTLE were a different breed, their values permanently changed. They had lived through the miseries of trench warfare, where pain and death were a commonplace. On the plus side, they had been exhilarated by victory, heartened by solidarity with men of other nations, and their first tastes of travel, the graces of elder civilizations and the more delicate charms of the mademoiselle from Armentieres left them with heightened sensibilities and liberalized attitudes.

Nor would medicine ever be the same for the returning doctors. They too had lived through the horrors and tasted of the good life. Many for the first time encountered regular hours, periodic furloughs and an assured, comfortable income. More important, the very gruesomeness of the war, the huge number of casualties and the necessity of ministering to them quickly and often radically, became an incalculable stimulus to medical advance. Physicians and surgeons rapidly accumulated a fund of experience that a lifetime of peacetime practice could not have supplied. Under the pressure of the battlefield, observations were made and correlated and new techniques devised and tested that would otherwise have taken generations to bring to fruition.

The doctors returned ready to place their new knowledge and expertise at the service of their civilian patients. In return, they expected to be decently paid. Patients, even the most grateful, rarely now responded with a side of venison or a bushel of fine apples. The cost of establishing and maintaining a practice had risen considerably. The income tax had not been repealed as expected. The doctor had to live, and he wanted to live well.

By and large, physicians were untrained and inexperienced in the ways of making money. However, many of them soon caught on. The legal prohibition of liquor allowed them an almost guaranteed income, for the moral desirability of prohibition was disputed and the demand for liquor was high. Each doctor was issued one hundred prescription blanks per month that were redeemable, when he signed and dated them, for one bottle of liquor each, to be used strictly for medicinal purposes. Some of the new post-war practitioners, short of patients and of money, simply signed all their presciptions at the beginning of each month and turned them over to the druggist, who waited, money in hand, ready to pay the going rate of three dollars per voucher. The more traditional members of the profession often were loud in their criticism of their "villainous" confreres. Little attention was paid to the rebuttal that few doctors in the province ever had an unused prescription at the end of the month.

But feuds within the ranks were not the only problems faced by the profession. During the war, when so many families had loved ones overseas and long casualty lists were published daily in the newspapers, there had been a revival of faith. At popular gatherings, congregations met to sing rousing hymns and listen to Bible-thumping oratory at its soul-saving best. The emotional power generated at these meetings was so great that susceptible "sinners" would be "seized by the Lord" and fall to the floor shouting, "Hallelujah! Hallelujah! Glory Hallelujah!" Some who had been ill professed to be cured after such contact with the Lord and certain revivalists seemed to have more power than others and were known as faith-healers. Such a one was the Reverend Doctor Price, who came to Vancouver and Victoria on several occasions in the early 1920's. His meetings were packed with several thousand believers each night. The sick, the halt, the lame, and the blind came by wheelchair, automobile, even by ambulance, and there were many miraculous "cures." The following extract from a front page article in the *Victoria Colonist* of April 14, 1923, illustrates a typical meeting:

A crowded church last evening witnessed a remarkable demonstration of divine healing at the Metropolitan Methodist Church, during the service conducted by Doctor C. S. Price, the evangelist. About 35 persons afflicted with various forms of disease and bodily ailments testified that the pain with which they had been suffering, had left them, as they cried with joy 'The Lord be praised, Hallelujah! Glory be to God.' One of the most outstanding cures was that of a dumb boy, who, after Doctor Price had prayed over him, said two words 'Praise' and 'Yes,' the great congregation manifesting its satisfaction by hearty applause, while many in the audience waived their handkerchieves and shouted 'praise to God.'

That all did not go well for Doctor Price is manifest by the headline in the *Colonist* of May 10th of the following year: "Price case engages City Police Commission without any decision being reached." The city fathers managed to bar further sessions of "divine healing," but it was an achievement against odds. Many of Price's strongly religious followers refused to believe documentary evidence that he was doing more harm than good with his so-called cures. They claimed that those who opposed Price were inspired by the devil himself — an argument difficult to refute calmly with reason and logic.

Although the practice of dentistry was becoming less and less painful, fear of the drill still beset the population. Potential dental patients were constantly on the lookout for a painless dentist. Thus, great interest was stirred by the arrival of a well-trained dental surgeon by the name of Parker. When he hung out his shingle his first name, which had been legally changed to "Painless," caught all eyes. A great showman, and interested in attracting a paying clientele, he set up a dental parlour at the corner of Columbia and Hastings Streets in Vancouver. To prove to the skeptics that he was a painless operator, he had a dental chair installed on a low platform in the front of his establishment, where the crowd from the street could gather round and watch him work. In the style of a side-show barker, he harangued the crowd as he claimed the ability to pull teeth without pain. The author, a medical student at the time, used to stand in the big crowd and watch him by the hour, impressed by his skill and showmanship as, after expertly doing regional nerve blocks with novocaine, he removed one by one the teeth of some poor derelict from the nearby Skid Road. After each removal, the tooth was held high in the air and shown to the crowd, and then a testimonial that he felt no pain demanded from and given by the bewildered patient. Painless Parker developed a thriving business and employed a number of dentists in his large dental parlour. The quality of the work turned out was said to be high.

The practice of medicine continued to advance. There had been a threat of a second epidemic of Spanish influenza, but the actual outbreak was not a serious one. There were the usual minor epidemics of infectious diseases, and sporadic flashes of smallpox still occurred. The last serious outbreak of the disease came in 1931 when 56 cases were reported in Vancouver, with 16 (28.5%) fatalities. The public health authorities responded by carrying on a campaign against the conscientious objectors to vaccination. Pictures were shown of three surviving members of one family who had been vaccinated and did not get the disease. The other four members, who were conscientious objectors, had died of smallpox. Typhoid fever was occurring less and less frequently, as people began to understand the grave dangers of drinking contaminated water.

Insulin had been discovered by Banting and Best, and work was progressing rapidly to purify the original crude extract, thus giving some hope to diabetics. The first vitamins had been isolated previous to the war and, as a wartime measure, P. A. Woodward[1] had added Vitamin D to the bread being baked for his department stores. Raw liver had been found to control pernicious anemia and was to lead quickly to the isolation of Vitamin B12 as a specific for the control of the deficiency state. Chlorosis was becoming a disease of the past and greenish wan young ladies no longer drank vinegar to satisfy a hidden thirst. The use of iodized salt was becoming commonplace and goitres were diminishing in number. The electric refrigerator had made its appear-

153

ance in a few homes, and was rapidly gaining in popularity as a means of preserving food and thereby raising the nutritional standards of the community.

The practice of medicine was carried on by the post-war doctors with new training, new ideas and new facilities. Blood transfusions were introduced as life-saving measures, though for a time they were used only as a last resort. The administration of one 500 cc. transfusion was considered a major therapeutic accomplishment and rarely was a second or third transfusion given, as is commonplace today. Before the simplified citration method for preventing the coagulation of blood came into use, there were several complicated and highly involved methods of getting the blood from the donor to the recipient. Multiple syringes, prepared with sodium citrate, were used in one method. The technique required that one doctor draw the blood from the donor in a syringe and pass it to his confrere, who injected it slowly into the vein of the recipient. In the meantime, the first doctor was filling another syringe full of blood from the donor and the process was repeated over and over until the required amount of blood was transfused. In another method, a mechanical pump sucked the blood from a donor and, when a valve was turned, pushed it into the recipient. The donor was paid a fee of twenty five dollars for his blood, but there were few offers, as most individuals were afraid of what might happen if they lost that amount of blood. Because of the scarcity of donors, the author in his boyhood was called upon in many an emergency and was delighted when he also received the fee. He was a practising physician fifty years later when one of the recipients came to his office to thank him once again for what she considered a great and unusual service rendered in time of dire need.

Diagnostic X-rays had been introduced, but their expense to the uninsured patient precluded many applications today taken for granted. This resulted in many missed diagnoses and inadequate treatment, all too often leading to unnecessary permanent disabilities. X-ray therapy was in its infancy and great hopes were held out that it would cure certain types of cancer. Because of the large doses administered, X-ray burns were sometimes almost as bad as the original disease. The patients were not the only ones burned, as in the early days the destructive effects of over-exposure were not well understood. Many doctors unwittingly overexposed themselves and developed malignancies in the skin of their fingers and hands, all too often requiring extensive and mutilating amputations.

The haematology and biochemistry laboratories were coming into their own and it was no longer necessary for the doctor to taste the urine to rule out diabetes. Bacteriology was coming to the fore also, and a use of autogenous immune serums was popular to combat the prevalent problems of such chronic infections as furunculosis, carbuncles, and others.

The treatment of women occupied a major portion of most doctors' time. Primarily, their problems centred about the "female organs" and the complications of childbirth. The doctors had assumed the task of delivering the babies and their efforts were considered an improvement over those of the midwife.[2] The delivery, however, continued to be done in the home, and perineal tears were common. Post partum, little attention was paid to the damaged area. Every woman was expected to have a large number of children and it was believed that a perineal repair was a waste of time until her child-bearing days were over. This assumption led to much suffering and unpleasantness. The torn bladder ligaments not only permitted the bladder to sag but also resulted in urinary frequency, and even incontinence. Often only the fact that the tissues were young and elastic prevented the condition from becoming intolerable. A torn perineum permitted the bulging of the rectum into the vaginal space, sometimes to the point were it protruded through the vulva. If the anal sphincter was torn, the poor woman suffered from fecal incontinence and, because satisfactory surgical repair was so difficult, she all too often became a psychological and physical recluse, afraid to mingle with others because of the constant smell of feces and the ever present danger of a serious "accident." The torn cervix of the uterus became eroded and infected, causing a most unpleasant vaginal discharge. The inflammation created an ascending lymphangitis that caused the woman to have a low backache. At times, the lymphangitis flared into a frank infection and the poor woman suffered from an acute pelvic inflammatory disease that, in their ignorance, the doctors frequently attributed to gonorrheal infection. The bulging rectum interfered with the normal function of the bowel and this, coupled with the infection, led to the cruel definition of a woman as a "constipated biped with a backache."

In these days, when some women are casting aside their brassieres as demeaning sex symbols, many doctors remember how frequently they once prescibed uplift brassieres to be worn twenty four hours a day, not as sex symbols but to relieve the pain of pendulous breasts of those who had never worn a support. To those doctors, the brassiere corrected an error made by nature when Homo sapiens arose and started to walk on hind legs. As a result, the centre of gravity of the female breast changed and, after the resiliency of youth was gone, the breast began to sag, often painfully disturbing the circulation of the blood to the milk gland structure, frequently with painful sequelae. To the non-medical perfectionist, the brassiere is a female sex symbol, not designed to stir the libido of man, but to enhance the beauty of Nature's complex curve compounded on curve that has made the female body so attractive as a thing of beauty to artists and sculptors for centuries.

When the menopause came, a woman's sex life was considered to be over. She was then admitted to hospital for the repairs that she had needed so badly for so long. In Vancouver the operation she was about to undergo was known among doctors as the "Trilby," after the popular novel of that name by Daphne Du Maurier. Trilby was a demure young lady who daringly posed in the nude for Svengali, disguising her shame by calling it the "all together." This last phrase succinctly described the broad range of surgical procedures to be done. They were quickly and efficiently carried out by the general surgeon of those days, though they sound far too drastic to be inflicted on an individual at any one time today. The patient was put in a lithotomy position with her feet suspended in the air. Diagnostic curettage was done to scrape out redundant mucous membrane and to determine the presence or absence of any potential malignancy. The cervix was then partially amputated and repaired to remove the infected areas. The bladder ligaments and the bladder were pushed back into place and resuspended normally. If the urethral sphincter was torn, a stitch was placed there to repair it. The perineum was then repaired and the rectum pushed back into its normal position, and any post-partum hemorrhoids removed. The patient was then lowered to the supine position, the abdomen opened, and the uterus examined. If it was considered necessary, the uterus, fallopian tubes and ovaries were removed. Otherwise, the tubes were ligated to prevent the remotest chance of further pregnancy and the uterus was suspended, as it was felt that any malposition of the uterus aggravated the backache. If the appendix was still there, that vestigial troublemaker was removed. The gall bladder was examined manually and, if stones were present and the area was not too inaccessible, the gall bladder was removed also. As an encore, after sewing up the abdominal incision, the surgeon took a small transverse-bladed knife known colloquially as a "spoke-shave" and scraped out the redundant mucous membrane in the nasal passages to relieve the chronic nasal congestion known as catarrh, so common in those days of poorly heated homes. As a final insult to the body, any carious teeth were extracted. The patient, bleeding from all orifices and with a burette full of normal saline solution dripping into a vein in her arm, was placed on a stretcher and trundled off to face the remaining years of her life free from the "female troubles" that had plagued her for so many years and secure in her mind that, as she grew older and her ligaments weaker, her female organs would not prolapse and hang between her legs as had happened to her mother before her.

For centuries women had been set apart from men because of the mysteries of their reproductive system. As young women they were subject to the recurring surges of hormones that controlled their menstrual cycle and at the same time created distressing maladies and labile emotions that were beyond the ken of the hormone-stable man. After the child-bearing period was over, the pull of gravity on their torn tissues and organs created more inhibiting ailments that further mystified the intact vigorous male, and so the "Trilby" type of surgical procedure can perhaps be considered a milestone in the process of freeing women from the fetters of their sex organs. As is so often the situation, once the first bonds were sundered successfully, others were quickly severed also. . . . The gynecologist soon controlled her hormones so that her menstrual cycle became more stable, and the obstetrician learned the value of protecting her supporting tissues at the time of delivery and immediately repairing any that were damaged. With this new found freedom from the trauma of her child bearing period, the stage was set for her final escape from the responsibilities of undesired pregnancies, and the liberated woman began to move out of her seclusion to share the day to day problems of existence with the remaining surviving males.

Doctors had other problems with women. In those days, when the virtue of woman was so highly prized and the belief that every man was a potential lustful beast so common, the unsupported word of the female was generally accepted as the final, incontrovertible proof of guilt of any man she wished to accuse. This placed the doctor in a dangerous position and it was considered mandatory for him to have his nurse at his side in a room with a female patient. The briefest departure from this rule could bring disaster in the form of character assassination or blackmail. An even more difficult situation to control was that of the so-called "badger-game." The author's father was caught by the stratagem on more than one occasion and considered himself lucky to escape with the mere forfeiture of the contents of his wallet. In the usual sequence of events, he would receive a late-night emergency call to some apartment. He would be told, as was common, that the door would be left unlatched. He would enter unsuspectingly and a voice would call him to the bedroom, where he would find a nude woman lying on the bed. At that moment, the "irate husband" would appear and accuse the doctor of attempted rape. The woman would verify the accusation. It was a difficult predicament. The doctor's reputation was on the line along with his legal position and many who tried to fight in court lost not only the judgment but their practices, as well.

The problem of cancer was a serious one and few diagnostic aids such as cytological smears and rapid section biopsies were available at that time. The diagnosis of carcinoma of the breast was made very late, at a stage that today is considered inoperable. The amputation of the breast, with a radical dissection of the muscles and the adjacent lymph gland, was considered so formidable that it was only done when the clinical diagnosis was absolutely certain. The criteria for operation were fixation of the tumour, dimpling of the skin, and/or enlarged, hard lymph glands in the axilla, signs that today usually indicate inoperability. Nevertheless, the meticulous, detailed, surgical procedure that was carried out at the time resulted in many cures. One woman who had her breast removed under such circumstances by the author's father outlived him and died forty-five years after her amputation without any recurrence.

The working male had his share of health problems. His wife and family depended on him for their "bread and butter" and, if he became ill, they would suffer along with him. If he had to stop work, he not only lost his wages but risked losing his job, as well, with the possibility of never finding another. The consequence was that he worked on from day to day, enduring whatever problems he had and often, as it were, dropping in harness.

Herniae and prolapsing hemorrhoids were still the major disabling problems of the labouring man. Both were aggravated by effort and each required painful, uncomfortable operations. Most of the best surgeons had learned from experience the great advantages of early ambulation, but many of the lesser, self-taught surgeons believed that long periods of post-operative rest in bed, followed by months of abstinence from any heavy physical effort, would tend to reduce the recurrence of hernia. This latter type of care was economically unfeasible for the average man and, combined with the unpleasantness of the anaesthetic, the pain of the operation and the post-operative sequelae, did not encourage him to submit to early surgery.

As he grew older and his prostate larger, he struggled manfully against the encroaching obstruction to urination and accepted his difficulties, much as his wife accepted her "female troubles." As time went on, his bladder became trabeculated and the ureters and kidneys dilated by the back pressure. Infection inevitably set in and increased the distress. Finally, the kidneys would deteriorate and waste elements begin to accumulate in his blood. From time to time, he would be unable to empty his bladder at all and an emergency call would bring the doctor, his trochar in hand. After percussing out the distended bladder and painting the skin area with a daub of iodine, he would plunge the sharp, pointed cannula through the lower abdominal wall — without any anaesthetic — into the bladder and relieve the man's distress.

The fear of prostatectomy was so great that men postponed the procedure until they had no further choice. By that time, the kidneys were so damaged that the nitrogen retention level in the blood was high. It was customary to decompress the bladder and rest the kidneys by making an incision just above the pubis, allowing the urine to escape freely. The decompression procedure was continued for several weeks and the male genito-urinary ward was recognizable from afar by its aroma of stale urine. When the surgeon considered the patient sufficiently strong to stand the operation, he enlarged the supra-pubic incision and enucleated the prostrate from above, very often removing glands that had grown from the size of a horse chestnut to that of a small apple. If there was any malignancy present, bleeding was a serious problem, and the patient frequently bled to death, no matter what was done for him.

Among the less acute problems of man in those times was one that still occasionally raises its head: to circumcise or not to circumcise. For millenia, the rite had been performed — sometimes for religious and presumably hygienic reasons, at other times as a ceremonial to mark the adolescence and maturation of the boy, and perhaps to prepare him for a long and happy sex life. This long-standing preoccupation with the male prepuce is illustrated in the religious paintings of the early artists. Christ on the Cross and many saints undergoing martyrdom were shown as having an infantile penis with a long tight foreskin. Apparently, this was considered a sign of virginity in the male. During intercourse, it would presumably be stretched and its appearance changed.

For whatever reason, the question of circumcision has been seriously debated by many young couples over the years. Few Vancouver doctors, however, doubted the wisdom of the procedure. After all, they were the ones called out in the middle of the night, in those days before super-clean babies became a fetish and the tight prepuce was prone to grow swollen and sore from moist smegmous inflammation. This quickly resulted in a high fever, urinary retention, a wailing baby and frantic parents, requiring the destruction of the virginally tight prepuce with a dorsal slit performed on the spot. Little wonder that many an experienced family doctor deliberately influenced the decision of a concerned young couple debating the circumcision of their newly arrived son and heir. The doctor would take the young father aside and, referring to the prevalent concern about the average male's precocious sexual sensitivity, whisper conspiratorially, one man of the world to another, "The end of the pecker should be so tough that a man could split wood with it." That usually settled the indecision of the master of the house and the virginal infant was deflowered forthwith.

The dictum laid down by Doctor Davie — that a diagnosis of appendicitis should be followed immediately by the removal of the appendix in an attempt to prevent the development of peritonitis — had generally been accepted. The death toll was still relatively high, compared to these days when antibiotics have so greatly reduced the danger of infection. An abscess became the occasion for considerable controversy as to whether the appendix should be removed as the nidus of infection or the abscess be allowed to contain itself and quieten down before surgery was performed, in the belief that this would lessen the chance of general peritonitis.

An experience of the author when he was little illustrates the extremes of surgery at the time. He was invited for dinner at the home of a young playmate. The author's father, learning of the invitation told his son that he could not go, explaining his decision only many years later: The playmate's father was a dedicated surgeon who believed implicitly in Dr. Davie's dictum and would let nothing stand in the way of what he considered the safety of his patient. Apparently, another little boy had gone there for dinner and, on complaining of some pain in his tummy during the postprandial period, was immediately taken into the adjoining surgery where an anaesthetic was administered and the appendix removed, before the boy was returned home to his parents.

The common and sometimes lethal consequences of spreading bacterial infections were a constant spectre looming over the practising doctor. In those pre-antibiotic days, every scratch, every minor wound, every pustule was carefully inspected and assessed by the physician, who was well aware of the deadly complications that could arise. Some infections remained localized. Others could spread with great rapidity through the system and snuff out the patient's life in short order. There was not a doctor who had not lost one or more of his colleagues following an apparently inconsequential needle prick or scratch. Though treated with iodine, it had permitted the entry of bacteria that took their fatal course within twenty four or thirty six hours.

The author's father was laid up for three months with an infected finger received from a needle prick at the time of an operation. He was fortunate that the consequences were not more serious. His son, in his turn, spent several months with a similarly infected finger. There was hardly a physician who had not some sort of infection or other, as a result of contamination from the wounds of his patient. The most impressive and frightening of all was that of gas gangrene. A simple puncture wound would permit the entry of the bacteria. Within hours, the subcutaneous tissues would be swelling and audibly crackling as the gas formed under the skin. The spread was so fast it could be clearly observed and, when death ensued, the body was a swollen mass, with the features distorted and movement visible and audible, as the gas-forming organisms continued their work. Such experiences with infection caused physicians to adopt progressively rigid regimes for the treatment of even the most minor laceration or infection.

The Twenties will be remembered for the first positive efforts to control tuberculosis. Till that time, when an active case had been laboriously diagnosed, usually as a result of the advanced ravages of the disease, the patient was sent to a sanatorium where he had to content himself with bed rest, fresh air and an adequate diet. All too often, these measures were sadly insufficient.

In Europe, experiments with the injection of air into the pleural cavity to collapse and rest the infected lung had produced remarkable results — if they could be believed. The medical profession of North America refused to accept the figures at first. It is to the credit of a Canadian, Doctor Norman Bethune, suffering from the disease and awaiting death in an American sanatorium, that he challenged the head of the institution to do a pneumothorax on him. The cure was prompt and remarkable. Dr. Bethune lived on to develop the art of transfusing blood to the point where it could be administered on the battlefields of the Spanish Civil War. The technique was to save many lives in the years that followed.

Doctor and Patient: An Overview

IT HAPPENED DURING WORLD WAR II, when the author was a young doctor in the Canadian Armed Forces, and concerned one of the first wartime casualties he was called upon to treat. The locale was the northern outpost city of Prince Rupert, a potential focal point for Japanese bombing. Rumours held it a likely beachhead, in the event of invasion.

In the circumstance, both the Army and the Navy occupied the town. Soldiers, rifles loaded, stood on guard over strategic areas, and even civilians had to give the password before they were permitted access. It irked some of the old-timers. The young soldiers, they felt, were taking the war a little too seriously. A few of the good citizens even went so far as to refuse to respond to the sentry's challenge. Inevitably, the odd bullet flew.

The casualty referred to was a dour old Scotsman and his case was unusual, in that it produced considerable trauma without drawing a drop of blood. The patient, a veteran of twenty years' work on the docks, had been on his way to work one morning when he was challenged as usual by the young sentry, who demanded that he halt and give the password. On this particular morning, for one reason or another, the old Scotsman had had enough of soldier-boy "nonsense." He continued on his way, even as the challenge was repeated. Having no alternative, the sentry fired, aiming low to avoid inflicting mortal harm. The target had turned sideways as he walked down the dock and the bullet, piercing the seat of his trousers, scorched its way across the skin of the cheeks of both buttocks and, exiting from the trousers, thereupon inflicted a similar burn across the palm of the victim's hand as it swung back in the motion of walking, passed along the thumb, and spent itself in the waters of Prince Rupert Harbour. Surgically, it was a minimal trauma; psychologically, the effect was somewhat greater. The man suffered from a substantial shock to the ego, and it was said that he never challenged authority again.

The event brought to the author's mind a somewhat earlier case of authority challenged. It concerned a man who had been severely injured in a traffic accident. His abdominal cavity had been torn open and subject to contamination, a condition that in a prior time would have ended in peritonitis and death. In addition, the man had been suffering from a gonorrheal infection that under extant treatment would have required several months to cure. The author, on duty in the wards, was presenting the case during rounds, and the attending doctors included a venerated and very senior physician. Pointing to the fully recovered patient, the young doctor was rash enough to attribute the dramatic cure to a new family of drugs — the sulfonamides. Whereupon the senior physician turned incredulously and remarked, "Doctor, you are a young man and have yet to learn there is no drug that will do what you have just claimed the sulfonamides will do. There will be no discussion. We will go on with the next case."

In this instance, too, the challenge to authority was answered with a bullet, albeit a verbal one. It was not the first time that such a projectile had been loosed at a young doctor's ego, nor would it be the last. More to the point, the blast was one of many of a similar sort, and they signalled the end of an era. For the introduction in the thirties of sulfonamide chemotherapy — soon to be followed by the first dramatic feats of penicillin and other antibiotics — dealt a mortal blow to the kind of medicine practised by many of the senior physicians. When such a mainstay of their practice as lobar pneumonia became almost extinct in a few months, when the treatment of so many other infectious diseases quickly became a matter of routine, these men saw a lifetime of careful training and meticulous observation going down the drain. And this was only one of several factors at work that were to transform the doctor's role in his world.

To understand how fate was catching up with the doctor it is well to return to the tight relationship of medicine and religion from which the doctor and his function originally sprang. It is a commonplace today to speak of the physician as concerned with the well-being of man's body and the priest as concerned with the well-being of his spirit. Underlying this differentiation of roles is the notion that the priest deals in the utility of faith while the physician deals in the utility of science. Such a view is a relatively recent development and is even today not wholly tenable.

That man, in the far reaches of pre-history, would look upon medicine and religion as a single entity is readily grasped. Any threat to his well-being that could not be warded off through his rudimentary fund of practical expedients called for the mysterious powers of the spirit doctor. And it was faith in those powers — whether employed in lulling the spirit of a hunted animal or in expelling the spirit of a painful carbuncle — that catalyzed whatever gains toward well-being were available to man through his own effort and determination. Even when, much later, the priest-physician lost his hyphen for much of mankind and his role was apportioned between clerical man and medical man, faith remained the essential tool of both. To be sure, practical aids to health and healing — herbal infusions, natural unguents, dietary laws, splints, compresses, occasionally even so complex a procedure as trephining — had been picked up along the way, but the most powerful agent in the medical man's bag remained his ability to invoke the patient's faith in cure, thus freeing the patient to mobilize his native defenses and recuperative drives. The doctor was, first and foremost, a master of psychosomatic medicine, an agent provocateur for the power of positive thinking.

It is sometimes forgotten how recently this state of affairs prevailed. Only in the last 200 years has medical research begun to accumulate a body of physiological and pathological data and techniques sufficient to affect materially the principles of health care. It has taken perhaps a hundred years more for these new principles of scientific medicine to pass in a tested and consolidated form into the hands of the practitioner, for day to day use with his patients. Even then, and well on into the twentieth century, the growing efficacy of his measures in dealing with an ever broadening range of ills served only to enhance his patients' faith in his apparently mystic powers — for science, to many a layman, remained ringed in magic and mystery. Little wonder then that at the turn of the century the family physician was at the height of his effectiveness and prestige. His patients looked on him with affection and respect and took his word for law. He, in turn, could take so great a satisfaction from this esteem and from his sense of usefulness that considerations of his own well-being and that of his family often became secondary in his mind.

The first crack in the family physician's image as a kindly and benevolent deity appeared with the advent of World War I and the forced transformation of medical practice into a money-making venture. In religious practice, the priest does not send out monthly statements (though a lower-echelon member of the hierarchy sometimes does!). Then, too, the layman before long began to lose some of his awe at the marvels of modern science. Little by little, he came to grasp some of the basic principles that underlay the advances of modern medicine. The more he learned, the less he ascribed to miracles.

As medicine grew in sophistication, so did the patient. As the major scourges of mankind began to bow before routine medical procedures, the patient began to expect cures for a host of hitherto undiagnosed or untreatable ailments, as well as for a large number of conditions which in the past he had dismissed as minor. Inevitably, the proliferation of diagnostic possibilities and available techniques began to overload the capacity of the all-around family practitioner. It was equally inevitable that, in the face of the growing overload, the practice of medicine would undergo fragmentation. From being doctors to the whole man, more and more physicians turned to becoming practitioners on people's parts. More and more, the term "family physician" became interchangeable with "referring physician," meaning someone concerned primarily with farming out problems to the appropriate specialists.

The age of specialization, the age of the medical "team" with its growing multitude of sophisticated and refined procedures, meant also an age of soaring costs. The feeling grew that the main burden of these costs ought not to be conferred on the hapless patients simply through the accident of his injury or ill health. Thus, in British Columbia as elsewhere in the world, the citizens, through their government, introduced a system of publicly financed health care that led to further changes in the role of the physician.

Today in British Columbia, the citizen is convinced of his *right to health*. Often the patient arriving at the doctor's office comes prepared with the tests he requires and the name of the specialist to whom he expects to be referred. He may even demand a specific course of treatment. If a surgeon is consulted, he is brought in as a highly skilled but narrowly defined technician, to provide an opinion or perform a procedure within his limited scope. Similarly with the other "parts doctors." They are artisans, much as the naval surgeons of Captain Cook's day were artisans.

Such a system of specialists and teams does possess certain merits. It allows for highly focused research and application. In time, we may expect some of the work currently underway in genetics, embryology and pediatrics to lead to significant break-throughs, breakthroughs that will allow the doctor finally to shift the focus of his concern away from the cure of disease to those measures that will prevent the disease from ever occurring.

But such an eventuality lies in the future. For the present, medical science has not yet eliminated disease, nor made cure a foregone conclusion. It would seem, then, that the atrophy of the religious component of medical practice may have been a trifle premature — that in the absence of a "perfect" medicine a powerful faith that can release the self-healing propensities of body and mind remains a desirable ally for doctor and patient alike.

That modern medical science has not inspired such faith in sufficient measure may be witnessed in cocktail party conversation and in the restless hopping from doctor to doctor that appears so often to accompany an ailment like some sort of extra-medical symptom. It is demonstrated, most dramatically at times, in the fear and despair with which many a patient views his stay in even the finest of modern teaching hospitals. It is as if — in the face of the superb skills of the "parts doctors" and the sophistication of the most up-to-date procedures for diagnosis and treatment — he remains uncertain as to where to place his faith.

"I want to be *taken care of*," he seems to say. "Who will take care of me?" It is an age-old cry, and the search for faith is its essence.

The answer which appears to be taking shape in several countries of Western Europe and elsewhere involves the reinstatement of the general family practitioner in the central role he once played. Public responsibility for health care has long been acknowledged in these countries. Now, recognizing the need in terms of faith and medical efficacy of placing someone in charge who will know and treat the whole patient, they are displaying a growing tendency to rescue the general practitioner from his function as a mere referral service and to place him at the head of the medical team. There, often in association with other "G.P.'s," supported by competent paramedical personnel and a wide range of technological services, he is free to "take care of" his patient. Thus adequately backed up, he need consult a specialist only in truly appropriate contingencies. He can then coordinate and integrate all findings with reference to the patient's total history.

Whatever course medical practice takes in British Columbia, the patient's question — "Who will take care of me?" — will need to be answered. For the doctor-patient relationship that contributed so much to the success of health care was historically a one-to-one affair. Such a relationship does not seem feasible between man and fragmented institution.

NOTES

1. The earliest explorers found evidence that some of the survivors of wrecked Japanese junks and Spanish merchantmen had married Indian women.

2. The tale of Hoei-Shin and his journey to and return from the unknown kingdom of Fusang was known to the early explorers. Details of the reputed voyage are given in *Inglorious Columbus* by Edward P. Vining (1885) and *Fusang, or the Discovery of America by Chinese Buddhist Priests in the Fifth Century* by Charles G. Leland (1875). A later review of the subject is to be found in Joseph Needham's *Science and Civilization in China*. The first two authors enumerate the arguments as to whether or not Hoei-Shin had in fact made the round-trip journey to the country known as Fusang and in the end tend to believe him. Needham points out in a lucid discussion that the violent arguments of those opposed to the possibility of the journey had so effectually destroyed the "facts" in favour of the voyage that there was no chance of their being resurrected. At the same time he describes many authenticated customs, beliefs, philosophies and artifacts that link the early culture of the Americas to Asia. He also claims that the basic argument that such return voyages were impossible in those early days has now been refuted by the westward voyage of Thor Heyerdahl on his raft and the eastward voyage of a twenty-three-year-old Japanese named Heri Kenichi who in 1962 crossed from Japan to San Francisco Bay single-

handed in a 19-foot sailing boat. Needham nevertheless concludes from the information he has gathered that the tale was probably a fabrication.

Before the negative conclusion regarding the Hoei-Shin controversy is accepted, a further factor deserves consideration, namely, the fidelity of the information made available in the translations. The arguments pro and con have been based on minute dissections of every descriptive phrase attributed to Hoei-Shin. It would seem that such profound analyses are not warranted in relation to material that has undoubtedly been exposed to many extraneous etymological deviations during the English translations of the German translators of the Chinese documents that were the Chinese records of an interpreter's translation of a non-Chinese Buddhist priest's story of the strange things he saw in a country that nobody believed existed. The reaction of the interpreter and the scribes who documented the story undoubtedly were tinged with incredulity, even as was the King of Siam who scoffed at the story some visitors to his court told him, that when water became cold it turned solid and could be walked upon.

Further support to the Hoei-Shin tale is given by a report from the Soviet news agency TASS that Leningrad scientists Lev Gumilev and Bronislav Kuznetsov claim to have evidence that the Asian geographers knew of the existence of the Americas at least as early as 1500 B.C.

3. *Haida Myths* by Marius Barbeau
   the Volcano Woman, page 9.

4. It seems that about the year 1639 the Japanese government had ordered all junks to be built with open sterns and large square rudders that made them unfit for ocean navigation. It was the government's hope in this way to confine the Japanese to their own islands. In bad weather the unwieldy rudders were soon washed away and the vessels fell into the trough of the sea and rolled their masts out. The Kuro Shiwo current then swept them at a rate of at least ten miles a day northwards towards the Aleutian Islands and then south along the coasts of what were to become Alaska, British Columbia and the United States. Some junks arrived with a few of their crew members still alive after a drifting voyage that averaged eight to ten months, the longest recorded being seventeen months. The junks were all Japanese and their wrecks, along with miscellaneous flotsam, were often washed up along the western coast of Canada and were the prime source of copper and iron for the natives.

5. The story of the men rescued by the *Llama* has been recorded as follows:

In 1883 a Japanese junk was wrecked on the west coast of Washington territory, in the immediate vicinity of Cape Flattery. Many of her crew had perished and several dead bodies were found headed up in firkins in customary Japanese style, ready for burial. Out of seventeen persons, the only survivors, two men and a boy were rescued from the Indians by the Hudson's Bay Company vessel *Llama,* Captain McNeal who took them to England touching at Honolulu on their way. Thence they proceeded to Canton where they arrived in 1836, and stopped with Karl Gutzlaff, who learned the language and intended to accompany them to Japan. In 1837 they left Macao in the American brig "Morrison" despatched by Clarence A. King from Yedo Bay to bear them home. Being fired upon, July 27, and prevented from landing, she sailed for Kagoisima, where being equally unsuccessful she finally returned with the men to Macao.

Japanese Wrecks Stranded and Picked Up Adrift in the North Pacific Ocean, Charles W. Brooks (1964) p. 11.

Unfortunately, it is not known whether the sailors were eventually returned to their homeland. Japan was still practising isolationism at the time. Under an imperial decree of 1637 a Japanese who had left his country and lived abroad was not allowed to return, death being the penalty for travelling abroad, studying foreign languages, introducing foreign customs, or believing in Christianity.

CHAPTER 3

1. This sudden plunge of the post-partum woman into cold sea water probably had many purposes, including cleanliness. An additional benefit that occurs to a medical mind is that the sudden cold immersion after the warming effort of the labour undoubtedly tend to contract all organs and systems including the flaccid uterus, in those days before the advent of ergot and pituitrin.

2. At a later date the proud native father fired a musket from a doorway to celebrate the birth of his child.

3. The Masai in Africa place leaves with deodorizing propensities under their arms and in their huts to counteract offensive smells.

4. The early settlers of British Columbia found the mosquitoes to be a great problem. A traveller who encountered mosquitoes in the Crimea, the Mississippi Valley, the Prairies and the Rocky Mountains is quoted as saying; "Reader, if you have never been in British Columbia, then I say you do not know anything about insect persecution, neither can you form the faintest idea of the terrible suffering foes so seemingly insignificant . . . are capable of

inflicting." Other settlers told of dogs and cows being killed by the mosquitoes, and one reputable gentleman maintained that he had in his possession at one time a cow whose tail had been "so bitten by these venomous beasts that it had dropped off."

5. *Legends of Vancouver,* Pauline Johnson (1912)
Siwash Rock, page 9.

CHAPTER 4

1. Many observers have remarked on the very apparent improvement in the physical appearance of the natives when they started to partake of the oolichan oil after a period of deprivation. (Personal communication with Mrs. Margaret Palmer who had lived in the Queen Charlotte Islands for many years and was familiar with the work of the missionaries and of their schools).

2. McKelvie personally reviewed part of the Buddhist priest's tale and concluded that they were quite possibly describing the pools of decaying oolichans in one part of their story.

CHAPTER 5

1. "A Case of Primitive Trephining," Dr. G. E. Kidd, F.R.C.S. *The Great Fraser Midden (1948)*

2. Dr. Gunn on Shamanism: *Totemic Medicine and Shamanism among the Northwest American Indians* (1966) pages 700-706.

3. The fever-reducing propensities of infusions made from the bark of certain trees are discussed in *The Pursuit of Intoxication,* Malcolm Andrew (1971) page 285.

CHAPTER 6

1. *Stories of Early British Columbia,* Dr. W. W. Walkem (1914) page 40.

2. The factor's invitation to the ordination of the shaman came from the white governor, in contrast to Dr. Walkem's, which came from Nim-Nim, the Indian chief. When questioned as to whether or not the Indians would welcome a stranger to the ceremony, the governor stated emphatically that if anyone dared to object he would immediately hang him "as high as Haman".

CHAPTER 8

1. Barbeau is the authority for the story of the activities of the shaman during the 1918 influenza epidemic.

2. Witchcraft Trial: *Vancouver Daily Province,* March 25, 1931.

3. When Cook arrived at Nootka he was presented with the mummified hand of a child and he believed that the Indians were indicating to him he should be eaten. Other than that, and the ritual biting and swallowing of human flesh by the shaman, there does not seem to be any real suggestion that human beings were sacrificed and eaten.

4. As Assistant Commissioner of the British Columbia Provincial Police, Mr. Clark was familiar with and understood the Indian's way of doing things. His story of the little black boy is related in: *Some Incidents of Indian Magic,* Cecil Clark (1963) pages 6-7.

PART TWO

CHAPTER 9

1. Apparently it had been accepted that Drake had reached the latitude of 48° or higher but at the time of the Oregon boundary dispute the question of latitude was debated and the decision was in favour of 43°. R. T. Bishop produces evidence that is strongly suggestive that the 49°-50° level may be the correct estimate of Drake's northernmost penetration. His reasoning includes the flow of ocean currents and the problem of navigation in the day when no chronometers existed and longitude was difficult to determine and latitude was reckoned with the use of a cross-staff. He also points out that the discipline of meticulous log keeping had not been accepted and the records for that reason were not too complete. In conclusion Bishop remarks that the Government of British Columbia became so convinced that Drake had reached the latitude of Vancouver Island that the highest peak on the Island was named after Drake's ship, *The Golden Hinde.*

The landing that Drake made at the furthermost reach of his voyage is thought to have been in the vicinity of Long Beach on the west coast of Vancouver Island. It was his naming of the territory as New Albion and his claim of it for his Queen that was the origin of England's claim to the coast. New Albion was shown as English territory on many early charts.

CHAPTER 10

1. Not only was Perez looking for the Northwest Passage but he was spying on the activities of the Russians — in particular as to whether or not they were poaching on Spanish territory. Aboard his ship were two priests who presumably were there to save any heathen soul they encountered as well as recording the voyage.

2. After Captain Cook was killed, his commanders completed the explorations assigned to them and sailed to China. There they were surprised to find the sea otter furs that they had treated so casually, highly prized by the Mandarins. Apparently the beautiful furs had been obtained for many centuries from Japanese traders who had contacts with the hunters of the sea otter skins in the Aleutian Islands and the Pacific coast of North America as far south as Northern California.

1. The urine tubs were kept full at all times and it is said that this was, in part, because of the belief that urine was particularly efficacious in extinguishing a fire, the dread of all sailors.

2. The name "Grog" was derived from the nickname of Admiral Edward Vernon of the West Indies Fleet who was called "Old Grogram" in reference to his waterproof cloak of that name. Vernon was concerned with the drunkenness among the sailors and after consulting with his surgeons issued an order in 1740 that stated in part: " . . . the respective daily allowance of half a pint a man for all your officers and ships company, be every day mixed with the proportions of a quart of water to every half pint of rum, to be mixed in a scuttled butt kept for the purpose, and to be done upon deck, and in the presence of the Lieutenant of the Watch, who is to take particular care to see that the men are not defrauded in having their full allowance of rum, and when so served to them in two servings in the day, one between the hours of ten and twelve in the morning, and the other between four and six in the afternoon." *Medicine and the Navy*, Christopher Lloyd and Jack L. S. Coulter, (1961) Vol. III, page 70.

3. For a discussion of the problems of scurvy from early days up to and including World War II see: *Medicine and the Navy*, Vol. III, pages 293-328.

4. The origin of the Barber-Surgeons lies in the medieval period. At that time the "Houses of Pity" cared for the sick and the permanently disabled. The clergy who were closely associated with these houses were forbidden to "exercise any form of surgery which involves cauterization of incision."

   As a result, the religious houses made use of their barbers, whom they employed to shave their tonsures and clip their hair, teaching them phlebotomy and other simple forms of surgery. Thus it was that the church's abhorrence of bloodshed led to the creation of the Barber-Surgeons. As the practitioners of "physik" at that time considered themselves to be in the priestly class they too professed to abhor the shedding of blood and for that reason looked down on the Barber-Surgeons as mere craftsmen. The barbers, in addition to doing surgery and providing for the tonsorial needs of the monks, also helped them to live up to their religious vows. At stated periods according to the tenets of their religious order, the monks were bled by the Barber-Surgeon and "minutus est" was the latin terminology descriptive of one who had undergone the operation, meaning that he had been "minutus sanguine," i.e. deprived of blood. One order prescribed such venesection five times yearly ("Prima est Septemberi etc. etc.")

5. There appear to have been two students named Archibald Menzies who attended the University of Edinburgh in the late eighteenth century. No places of origin are given in their records and the only distinguishing feature is in the signatures, which are somewhat different. The following are the records of the classes they took:

Archibald Menzies I	1771/2	Anatomy and Surgery; Practice of Medicine.
	1772/3	Anatomy and Surgery; Practice of Medicine.
	1773/4	Anatomy and Surgery; Chemistry; Botany; Clinical Lectures.
	1774/5	Anatomy and Surgery; Theory of Medicine; Practice of Medicine; Pharmacy, Botany; Clinical Lectures.
Archibald Menzies II	1776/7	Botany.
	1777/8	Botany.
	1778/9	Anatomy and Surgery; Chemistry.
	1779/80	Botany; Anatomy and Surgery; Practice of Medicine; Infirmary.

Their Professors:

Anatomy and Surgery	Alexander Munro, Secundus.
Botany	John Hope.
Chemistry	Joseph Black.

Practice of Medicine .... John Gregory to 1773 and
afterwards Wm. Cullen.

Theory of Medicine .... Wm. Cullen 1773/76 James
Gregory; afterwards
Andrew Duncan, Primus.

A study of the signatures seems to indicate that Menzies Secundus was the one who became the surgeon on Captain Vancouver's *Discovery*. Many of the sea surgeons started as sick bay attendants and acquired their knowledge by practical experience. Most of them were young when they started and were known as "loblolly boys" because of the gruel of that name that they served to the sick.

6. The sea surgeon wore an identifying button on his jacket with the anchor and serpent device from the seal of the Sick and Hurt Board on it. This device was unofficial at first but was officially recognized in 1825.

7. MacKay sometimes called himself doctor but he probably did not have a doctorate of medicine. He was listed as surgeon's mate and Strange always referred to him in his writings as "Mister."

8. Moziño was not listed as surgeon on Bodega y Quadra's expedition and it is difficult to say whether he abstained from doing any medicine whatsoever. There was at least one other surgeon in the squadron — Louis Galvez, on the frigate *Aranzaza*.

CHAPTER 12

1. Poem from: *A Short History of Nautical Medicine*, Louis H. Roddis, (1941).

2. Home was an able seaman promoted to masters mate. His log is quoted in: *The Journals of Captain James Cook*, J. C. Beaglehole, (1967) Vol. III, Part II, page 1455.

3. Spruce beer became a popular "cure" for scurvy following Jacques Cartier's experience during his first winter in Eastern Canada (1535-36). Most of his crew became sick (and some died) of a strange malady and it was the Indians who showed him their cure for the disease — spruce beer.

CHAPTER 13

1. Moziño noted that the natives living in the small settlements around Nootka " . . . are gradually weakened by the ravages of venereal disease."

2. Cook's statement as to the cure rate in venereal disease: *The*

Journals of Captain James Cook, J. C. Beaglehole, (1967), Vol. III, Part I, page cxxi.

3. Cook's statement: *The Journals of Captain James Cook,* Vol. III, Part II, page 1534.

4. Samwell's statement: *The Journals of Captain James Cook,* Vol. III, Part II, page 1095.

5. Samwell's statement: *The Journals of Captain James Cook,* Vol. III, Part I, page 1178.

6. Driver's statement: *A Voyage around the World, but More Particularly to the North West Coast of America,* Captain George Dixon, (1789), page 295.

CHAPTER 14

1. It is interesting to note that, after centuries of devastating epidemics of smallpox, in 1970 there was hardly a single case of the disease reported from any of the western countries.

2. The Russian explorer Baranoff lost one hundred of his men from mussel poisoning.

3. Description of mussel poisoning: Public Records Office (PRO) Chancery Lane, London, England.

4. Even today the stapholococcus is the scourge of the surgical wards. It causes a persistent infection and is difficult to control even with modern drugs.

5. Moziño's statement on rats: *Noticias de Nutka,* J. M. Moziño, page 7.

CHAPTER 15

1. The use of the lash had been curtailed to some extent towards the end of the eighteenth century. Previously it had been used indiscriminately and often brutally. In addition to the ordinary lashing as described, a sailor on conviction for a serious offense could, when the ship was in harbour, be "lashed around the fleet." He was secured to an upright grating on a barge and then taken to each ship in the fleet in turn and then to the tune of the Rogues March given so many lashes in front of the assembled crew. Often the victim was nearly dead before he completed the round but the procedure was either temporarily postponed until he recovered or the corpse was given the lashes required before each of the remaining ships. The punishment of the lash fell into disrepute in the nineteenth century. About mid-century it's

179

purpose as punishment was often defeated by young men who were able to accept the lash without an outcry, inspiring their fellow sailors to do the same.

CHAPTER 18

1. As a candidate for the surgical diploma of the Royal College of Surgeons of Edinburgh, Kennedy was required to have studied in some university or school of medicine of reputation:

> Under Professors in such University, or under teachers who are Fellows or Licentiates of the Colleges of Physicians or Surgeons of London or Dublin, Fellows of the Colleges of Physicians or Surgeons of Edinburgh, or Members of the Faculty of Physicians and Surgeons of Glasgow, and who are resident within the precincts of the College or Faculty to which they respectively belong.
>
> Every Candidate must produce Certificates of his having attended the Instruction of the above designed Teachers for a period of three or more Winter Sessions, in the course of which time he must have attended the following separate and distinct Courses of Lectures:

ANATOMY	2 Courses
CHEMISTRY	1 do
MATERIA MEDICA	1 do
INSTITUTIONS OR THEORY OF MEDICINE	1 do
PRACTICE OF MEDICINE	1 do
PRINCIPLES AND PRACTICE OF SURGERY	1 do
MIDWIFERY	1 do
PRACTICAL ANATOMY	1 do

> The Candidate must likewise have attended a Public Hospital for at least one year, with a Course of Clinical Surgery during the period of his Hospital attendance.
>
> Though, by the present Regulations, it is not made imperative that Candidates for Surgical Diplomas should have attended a Course of Lectures on Clinical Medicine, the College earnestly recommend all Candidates to avail themselves of this valuable mode of practical instruction, as well as of that which, on similar principles, is derived from attendance at Dispensaries.
>
> The College would also impress on Candidates for Surgical Diplomas the advantages to be obtained from a Course of Practical Chemistry and Pharmacy, which seems to bear the same important relation to the science of Chemistry, as Dissection or Practical Anatomy does to the science of Anatomy.
>
> The duration of the Course of Study of Apprentices, whose Indentures commenced before 1st January 1823, remain unaltered.

A diploma of the Royal College of Surgeons did not entitle the use of the prefix "doctor."

2. The records of the University of Glasgow reveal that Tolmie attended there for a short period. He was awarded first prize in the chemistry class for second year students for "the best appearance at the public examination during the session" (1830-31). He

did not graduate with an M.D. and the university did not at that time award a "Diploma" in medicine.

3. The procedure of stopping the bleeding of severed artery by torsion is known as arteriostrepsis. The divided end of an artery is seized with a forcep and twisted, making two or three revolutions in the direction of its long axis causing a rupture and retraction of the two inner coats within the outer coat. This procedure is still used today by many surgeons.

CHAPTER 19

1. The *Blossom* served two commissions in South American waters, Peter McDougall acting as surgeon for the second. In 1825, the ship was commissioned again for a survey and exploratory voyage under Captain Beechy to the North Pacific and the Bering sea to explore some unknown territory and finalize the search for the Northwest Passage. During this commission she passed through British Columbia.

2. In 1852 Governor Douglas was alarmed by word that four vessels carrying some five hundred and fifty adventurers plus crews had sailed in the Queen Charlotte Islands for Gold Harbour. He believed that the history of American expansion in the previous two decades supported amply his contention that the lawless "floating population of California" would operate virtually with a free hand in the gold fields unless the authority of the Crown was strengthened by a show of British power. The frigate *Thetis*, thirty eight guns, under Captain Augustus L. Kuper, was dispatched from Callao to the Northwest coast and specifically to the Queen Charlotte Islands. Complemented by the paddle-wheel sloop *Virago*, six guns, under Commander James C. Prevost, the Navy "showed the Flag" and the mission was accomplished.

3. The most likely cause of aortic ulceration is syphilis in its tertiary stage. To have reached this level in a man so young he probably would have had to be infected in his immediate post-pubescent period — an assumption that would fit in to the code of morals and the way of life of a young sailor who joined the navy at an early age.

CHAPTER 20

1. On April 14th, 1871, it was noted in the British Columbia Directory: "At Newestminster, left without a doctor since the death of Doctor Black, late in March, was seeking a replacement. The practice, worth $5000 a year including $1000 from the jail

and hospital, covered the territory from Sand Heads to Yale including Burrard Inlet."

2. Griffith quoted: *The Medical History of British Columbia*, Dr. A. S. Monro, (1931-32), page 34.

3. Quotation from: *British Columbia from the Earliest Time to the Present*, F. W. Howay, E. V. S. Schofield, page 607.

4. Cridge quoted: *The History of British Columbia*, Dr. A. S. Monro, (1931-32).

5. Dr. Helmcken quoted: *Pioneer Doctor John Sebastian Helmcken*, M. Honor Kidd, (1946).

6. Emily Carr quoted: *The Book of Small*, Emily Carr, (1942).

PART FOUR

CHAPTER 24

1. The author received his first clinical lecture at an early age as he sat beside his father in the front seat of the Overland car, stopped at an intersection. A prominent Vancouver citizen was walking past and the good doctor pointed out his gait as characteristic of "Tabes Dorsalis" — a manifestation of the third stage of syphilis. Thereafter the boy was able to recognize the typical gait and soon learned that the disease was more or less commonplace and no respecter of wealth or of station.

2. The story of the English entrepreneur was told by the late Dr. Frank M. Bryant.

3. During American prohibition days, rum running was a major industry in and around Victoria. The law and the hijacker were ever-present enemies of the rum runner, and the latter used many subterfuges to evade them. One of them was the use of the leper colony island as a hidden storage depot for his reserve supply of liquor, the average man's dread of leprosy serving to bolster security.

CHAPTER 26

1. Mr. Woodward was always interested in the health of the citizens of his province. It was this interest that led him, when he first heard of the isolation of Vitamin D, to visit the discoverers. He was so convinced of its value that, as a health-preserving measure, he added the vitamin to the bread being baked in his stores. He never lost interest in health matters and made several large

donations that helped initiate the University of British Columbia Health Sciences Centre. Because of his respect for the pioneer medical men of British Columbia he had built and furnished the Charles Woodward Memorial Room, dedicated to the pioneer physicians of British Columbia and situated in the Woodward Bio-medical Library. He then proceeded to collect historical medical books from all over the world, placing them in the Memorial Room so that they would be available to coming generations. This collection is one of the finest of its kind in North America.

2. Dr. W. C. McKechnie in his time delivered over five thousand babies, mostly in the home. He carried all he needed in his little black bag and his sterilization technique consisted chiefly of boiling his instruments on the kitchen stove. If available, a neighbour woman was his assistant. The anaesthetic was administered by the patient herself, who was given some gauze soaked in chloroform. She was told to take deep breaths as the pains came and as the quick acting chloroform took effect, her hand fell away, whereupon she recovered, to repeat the performance from time to time as needed.

BIBLIOGRAPHY

Anderson, Bern: *Surveyor of the Sea*. Toronto, University of Toronto Press, 1960.

Ayyar, A. V. Venkatarama: *James Strange's Journal and Narrative of the Commercial Expedition from Bombay to the Northwest Coast of America*. Reprinted by Superintendent Government Press, Madras, 1929, pp. 21-22.

Bancroft, H. H.: *The Works of Hubert Howe Bancroft*, Vol. xxxii, *History of the Northwest Coast*, Vol. i, San Francisco, A. L. Bancroft & Co., 1884.

Barbeau, Marius: *The Siberian Origin of Our Northwest Indians*. Proc. Fifth Pacific Science Congress, Canada, 1933. Toronto, Vol. iv, 1934.

Barbeau, Marius: *Alaska Beckons*. Caldwell, Id., Caxton Printers, 1947.

Barbeau, Marius: *Medicine Men of the North West Pacific Coast*. National Museum of Canada, Bulletin No. 152, Anthropological Series No. 42.

Barbeau, Marius: *Pathfinders in the North Pacific*. Caxton Printers, 1958.

Beaglehole, J. C.: *The Journals of Captain James Cook*. Cambridge University Press, 1967.

Bell, Sir Charles: *The Religion of Tibet*. London, Oxford University Press, 1931.

Billings, Dr. John S.: *The History and Literature of Surgery.* Philadelphia, Lea, 1895.

Bishop, Capt. R. P.: *Drake's Course in the North Pacific.* Victoria, B.C. Historical Quarterly, July 1939, Vol. iii.

Boas, Franz: *The Social Organization and the Secret Societies of the Kwakiutl Indians.* From report of U.S. Museum for 1895.

Boas, Franz: *Kwakiutl Culture as Reflected in Mythology.* New York, American Folklore Society, G. E. Stechert & Co., 1936.

Boas, Franz: *Kwakiutl Ethnography.* Chicago, University of Chicago Press, 1966.

Boas, Franz: *Kwakiutl of Vancouver Island.* The Jessup North Pacific Expedition, Memoir of the American Museum of Natural History — New York, Vol. v, Part ii.

Brooks, Charles Wolcott: *Japanese Wrecks Stranded and Picked Up Adrift in the North Pacific Ocean.* Fairfield, Wash., Ye Galleon Press, 1964.

Carrington, Philip: *The Early Christian Church.* Cambridge University Press, 1957, Vol. ii.

Clark, Cecil: "Some Incidents of Indian Magic." *The Daily Colonist* — Islander Magazine, 23 June, 1963.

Copeland, Dr. Jas.: *Dictionary of Practical Medicine.* London, Longman, Brown, Green & Longman, 1844-58, Vol. i.

Curtis, L. Colin: "The Mosquitoes of British Columbia." Victoria, Occasional Papers of the British Columbia Provincial Museum, March 1967, No. 15.

Darby, Dr. G. D.: "The Mongolian Spot in British Columbia Coast Indians . . . . " Museum and Art Notes, December 1930.

Dixon, Captain George: *A Voyage Around the World but More Particularly to the North West Coast of America,* 2nd Edition, George Goulding Publishers, Covent Garden, 1789.

Edelstein, Ludwig: *The Hippocratic Oath.* Baltimore, The Johns Hopkins Press, 1943.

Farsy, Muhammed Saleh, *Islam and Hygiene.* Janus LI, pp. 81-124.

Fisheries Research Board of Canada. Bulletin No. 89.

Garrison, Fielding H.: *An Introduction to the History of Medicine.* Philadelphia & London, W. B. Saunders Co., 1929.

185

Godwin, George: *Vancouver A Life.* New York, D. Appleton & Co., 1931.

Goodfellow, Rev. John C.: "Religion in British Columbia Before the White Men Came." *Washington Archaeologist*, August 1959.

Goodfellow, Barry M. *The Royal Navy and the Northwest Coast of America, 1810-1914.* Vancouver, University of British Columbia Press, 1971.

Griffin, George: *Legends of the Evergreen Coast.* Vancouver, B.C., The Clarke & Stuart Co. Ltd., 1934.

Gunn, Dr. Sisvan W. A.: "Totemic Medicine and Shamanism Among the Northwest American Indians." *Jour. American Medical Association*, May 23, 1966, Vol. 196, No. 8.

Howay, F. W.: *Voyage of the Columbus to the Northwest Coast, 1787-1790 and 1790-1793.* Boston, Mass., Historical Society, 1941.

Howay, F. W. and Schofield, E. V. S.: *British Columbia from the Earliest Times to the Present.* Vancouver, S. J. Clarke Publishing Co.

Hyslop Jr., Newton E.: "Ear Wax and Host Defence." *The New England Journal of Medicine*, Vol. 284, No. 19, 13 May, 1971.

Johnson, Pauline E.: *Legends of Vancouver.* The Thomson Stationery Company, Vancouver, B.C., 1912.

Jones, W. H. S.: *The Doctors Oath.* Cambridge, at the University Press, 1924, Vol. I.

Keevil, J. J.: *Medicine and the Navy.* Edinburgh/London, E. & S. Livingstone Ltd., 1957.

Kidd, Honor M.: "Pioneer Doctor John Sebastian Helmcken." The Sir Wm. Osler Essay read before the Osler Society, McGill University, Montreal, Quebec, October 1946.

The Journal Lancet. London, 1867 ii, p. 95.

Large, Dr. R. G.: *Skeena — River of Destiny.* Vancouver, B.C., Mitchell Press Ltd., 1957.

Larsel, Olof: "An Outline of the History of Medicine in the Pacific Northwest." *Northwest Medicine*, Aug.-Dec. 1932.

Lehner, Ernest & Johanna: *Folklore and Odyssey of Food and Medicinal Plants.* New York, Tudor Publishing Co., 1962.

Leland, Chas. G.: *Fusang or the Discovery of America by Chinese Buddhist Priests in the Fifth Century.* London, Trubner & Co., 1875.

Lloyd, Christopher: *The British Seaman*. London, Granada Publishing Co., 1968.

Lloyd, Christopher and Coulter, Jack L. S.: *Medicine and the Navy.* Edinburgh & London, E. & S. Livingstone Ltd., 1961, Vols. iii & iv.

McKechnie Sr., Dr. R. E.: *Medicine.* See Howay, F. W. and Schofield, E. V. S.: *British Columbia, from the Earliest Times to the Present.* Vancouver, S. J. Clarke Publishing Co., Vol. i.

McKelvie, B. A.: "Maquinna the Magnificent." The *Vancouver Province*, 1964.

McKelvie, B. A.: "Magic Murder and Mystery." Duncan, B.C., *Cowichan Leader*, 1966.

McKelvie, B. A.: *The Pageant of B.C.* Toronto, Thomas Nelson & Sons, 1957.

Malcolm, Andrew: *The Pursuit of Intoxication.* Toronto, Thorn Press, 1971.

Monro, Dr. A. S.: "The Medical History of British Columbia." *The Canadian Medical Association Journal*, 1931-1932.

Moziño, Jose Mariano: *Noticias de Nutka.* Translated by Wilson, Iris Higbie, Toronto/Montreal, McLelland & Stewart Ltd., 1970.

Needham, Joseph: *Science and Civilization in China.* Cambridge University Press, 1971, Vol. 4, Part 3, pp. 540-553.

Niblack, Albert Parker: "The Coast Indians of Southern Alaska and Northern British Columbia." Report of the U.S. National Museum, 1888.

Osler, Sir William: *The Evolution of Modern Medicine.* New Haven, Yale University Press, 1921.

Pope, Dudley: *England Expects.* London, Weidenfeld and Nicolson, 1959.

Public Records Office (PRO). Chancery Lane, London, England.

Rickart, T. A.: "The Use of Iron and Copper by the Indians of British Columbia." *British Columbia Historical Quarterly*, 1939, Vol. iii.

Robbins, Rossell Hope: *The Encyclopedia of Witchcraft and Demonology.* New York, Crown Publishers Inc., 1965.

Roddis, Louis H.: *A Short History of Nautical Medicine.* London/New York, Paul B. Hoeber Inc. 1941.

Teit, James: *Ethnobotany of the Thompson Indians of British Columbia.* Washington Government, 1930.

Tolmie, William Fraser: *The Journals of William Fraser Tolmie, Physician and Fur Trader.* Vancouver, Mitchell Press Ltd., 1963.

The Great Fraser Midden. Vancouver Art, Historical and Scientific Association, 1948.

Vining, Edward P.: *Inglorious Columbus, or Evidence that Hwui Shan and a Party of Buddhist Monks from Afghanistan Discovered America in the 5th Century.* New York, D. Appleton & Co., 1885.

Wagner, Henry R.: *Spanish Voyages to the Pacific Northwest in the 16th Century.* San Francisco, California Historical Society, 1929.

Wagner, Henry R.: *Cartography of the Northwest Coast.* Berkeley, Calif., University of California Press, 1937, Vol. i.

Walkem, Dr. W. W.: *Stories of Early British Columbia.* Vancouver, News Advertiser, 1914.

INDEX